PANORAMA
OF EVIL

CONTRIBUTIONS IN PHILOSOPHY

Leonard W. Doob

PANORAMA OF EVIL

Insights from the Behavioral Sciences

CONTRIBUTIONS IN PHILOSOPHY, NUMBER 10

GP

GREENWOOD PRESS

WESTPORT, CONNECTICUT • LONDON, ENGLAND

ACKNOWLEDGMENTS

The quotation on pp. 52-53 is from *The Mountain People*. Copyright © 1972 by Colin Turnbull. Reprinted by permission of Simon & Schuster, a Division of Gulf and Western Corporation.

The quotation on pp. 53-54 is from *A Piece of Truth* by Amelia Fleming. Reprinted by permission of the publisher, Houghton Mifflin Company.

The quotations on pp. 60-61 are reprinted from *The Prophet*, by Kahlil Gibran, with permission of the publisher, Alfred A. Knopf, Inc. Copyright 1923 by Kahlil Gibran; renewal copyright 1951 by Administrators C.T.A. of Kahlil Gibran Estate, and Mary G. Gibran.

Library of Congress Cataloging in Publication Data

Doob, Leonard William, 1909-
    Panorama of evil.

    (Contributions in philosophy ; no. 10 ISSN 0084-926X)
    Includes bibliographical references and index.
    1. Good and evil. I. Title.
BJ1401.D66   216   77-87964
ISBN 0-313-20030-0

Library of Congress Catalog Card Number: 77-87964
ISBN: 0-313-20030-0
ISSN: 0084-926X

First published in 1978

Greenwood Press, Inc.
51 Riverside Avenue, Westport, Connecticut 06880

Printed in the United States of America

10 9 8 7 6 5 4 3 2 1

TO MY FRIENDS
IN CYPRUS
AND ELSEWHERE

CONTENTS

PANORAMA
OF EVIL

PROLOGUE

No matter where we look—in the past, the present or into the future—evil appears. It is difficult, usually impossible, to dip into a collection of proverbs from any society and not find bits of wisdom pertaining to its cause or cure. Every human being and every religion copes with "the riddle" of evil.[1] Christians from the very outset have striven to quell their doubts about God's goodness since He permits evil or about His power since He does not eliminate it.[2] Jesus cried out as He endured the pain and anguish of evil on the cross: "Lord, Lord, why hast thou forsaken me?" Imperfections in man leading to evil are universally recognized.

Probably almost everyone considers torture evil and can point to a particularly horrifying manifestation. But people still torture one another. Virtually every country contains individuals who literally mutilate those in their power: the secret police who would have prisoners confess or reveal information they would try to conceal, the sadist or the maniac who derives pleasure from the sight of pain. The violation of the human body is basic and virtually unendurable in a physiological sense, but our most private egos can also be invaded by taunts, insults, innuendos. Prisoners of authoritarian regimes and unhappy marriages are made miserable and often seek not to survive. Why, why does torture persist?

Evil is a central, baffling theme not only of theology but also of philosophy or any other discipline concerned with man. "Western ethical thought," one philosopher asserts, "has made little progress since the days of the Greeks."[3] A philosophical sociologist is even more crushing: "The subject that learned men call ethics is a wasteland on the philosophical map."[4] Political leaders who would be statesmen must give battle in behalf of what they choose to call good and against suffering, injustice, and other forms of abstract or concrete evil—and a few of them worry about mankind as well as their own constituents. Physicians of the body easily identify the evils they would conquer: disease and death. And the rest of us, anywhere, anytime, cannot live on without realizing that some men commit evil deeds and that every man probably contains within himself a mixture of good and evil.

The speculations, outcries, and treatises about evil, some produced by the outstanding sages of all times, obviously cannot be collated by one person, no matter how conscientious he or his computer strives to be. Is one not incredibly conceited or seriously deluded if he feels he can possibly add anything new or important to what has already been accumulated concerning evil? I cannot answer the question. Let me digress. Like everyone else, I have felt and know evil. For two years as an extraordinarily immature graduate student in Germany, I watched the Nazis organize and campaign until eventually, shortly after I returned to America, they successfully seized power. The hatred that they expressed and on which they thrived, I thought, personified evil according to the value system I had then and still retain. During World War II, I participated officially in psychological warfare, a form of activity that in large part disseminates evil against evil, although what we said and what we did we thought true and good. Toward the end of the colonial days in Africa, I was a harmless researcher and there could not prevent myself, again and again, from seeing Europeans maltreat Africans or sneer at their capabilities. Why should we act differently? they said. What should we expect otherwise when, after all, these black men not long ago were swinging from trees and were incapable of inventing the wheel or a system of writing? In my own country as well I have perceived what is glibly but accurately called man's inhumanity to man. Within myself I have not been devoid of emotions whose presence I despise: jealousy, selfishness, greed, dogmatism, as well as petty feelings and hatred regarding not the qualities of other persons but their personalities in general.

The final experiences driving me to grapple with evil were on Cyprus. There, on Aphrodite's beautiful birthplace, I participated during the first half of 1974 in the two communities, the Greek and the Turkish, which had so many common ties, which to some extent were striving to forget past enmities, but which continued to perpetuate mistrust arising less from what they themselves but more from what their ancestors had endured. What prevented them from living together in peace and harmony? In July of that year from the window of my flat, I watched with horror first the killing of Greeks by Greeks and, five days afterward, the exploding bombs from the Turkish planes swooping down from an innocent sky. Later, as I was driven in an automobile convoy toward the safety of a British base and as I saw the fertile fields denuded by what I was told had been napalm bombs, I had to wonder—once again, and this time perhaps more profoundly than on other occasions—why evil exists and whether it might not be, if not eradicated, at least diminished. Less than a year later and again after a year and a half and two years, I returned to Nicosia, the capital of Cyprus. No political solution was in sight. Thousands of refugees felt hopelessly separated from their homes, and tales of atrocities and cruelties were close to the surface of all conversations, at least in my presence. Evil, no matter how defined, seemed to be victorious.

As a result of these experiences I have been unable to prevent myself from thinking about evil, from reading what the sages have written, from consulting the wisdom in proverbs and other oral traditions, and from writing this book. What I am trying to do in these pages is to offer a panorama of the problems associated with the existence, the prevention, and the combating of evil. I provide no modern version of the Ten Commandments, Confucian Analects, the *Communist Manifesto*, or the *Critique of Pure Reason*; I would not contradict the prophets. Instead I would delineate what I believe we need to know or heed to cope with the natural and man-made plagues in the midst of which we perforce dwell.

Naturally I feel humble when I consider what has been said about evil and how the truly great—Aristotle, Plato, St. Augustine, Shakespeare, Goethe, Cervantes, Dante—have gracefully and attractively expressed the very relevant profundities. Is there anything new to add or subtract? I take courage from the belief that twists here and there in a modern idiom to a subject as ancient and important as evil might somehow provide new insights and hence be useful. The twists come from the social sciences and psychology. I must quickly note that the subject of evil, however, has scarcely been acknowledged as such by the professionals in these disciplines.[5] It is almost impossible to find an entry for "evil" in the recognized sources, such *Psychological Abstracts* and *Sociological Abstracts*; and a volume that purports to summarize the best generalizations in all the social sciences does not even mention the subject, in fact has pathetically few entries in its index even for the related problem of "values."[6]

But many of the findings of the scientific disciplines can help us to understand evil, although the word is not mentioned, and they will be discreetly cited. I say "discreetly" because of the limited generalizability of findings in the social sciences. It has been persuasively argued, for example, that the analysis of key concepts—intelligence, perception, group behavior, and the ego—could have been markedly affected by the historical age in which the analyst has happened to live.[7] Current theories on these topics would have been quite different if they had been formulated during the time of classical Greece, the Middle Ages, or the Renaissance, and research would have correspondingly varied. I deliberately employ two devices, therefore, to denigrate the professionals politely. First, notes are inconspicuously relegated to the end of each chapter. Second, sentences reporting results from a particular empirical or experimental investigation contain the word *may* or *perhaps* in italics to suggest that a generalization is derived from a limited sample of mankind and perforce from utilizing a specific method (including undocumented intuition) and is, therefore, limited in scope or significance.

My basic assumption is that what we call evil does not exist in nature the way mountains spring up across a landscape or hair grows on the human head. Nothing is evil—not even an earthquake, an atomic bomb, or a mass murder—until someone calls it that. The distinction between evil and any of its many antonyms, it has been suggested, would not be made if there were no life on this planet or only a single person.[8] Even when a specific evil is attributed not to contemporary antagonists, but to "history," reference is really being made to some identifiable or nonidentifiable individuals in the past.[9] Basically, therefore, we are dealing first of all with human judgments, the way we judge an object to be hot or cold, a person short or tall, a political party conservative or radical; and second with ways to improve human beings, to provide them with therapeutic suggestions.

No elaborate cast of characters is required. Individuals, it is clear, can be relegated to one or more of these three roles: *Judges*: persons possessing values and expressing value judgments concerning evil; *Evildoers*: persons committing evil as judged by others or themselves; and *Victims*: persons experiencing the effects of what is judged to be evil. An additional term is needed; *Situations*: circumstances in the environment judged evil because they produce or help produce Evildoers or Victims or both. (Throughout the discussion Judges, Evildoers, and Victims are capitalized to call attention to the somewhat specialized way in which the concepts are being employed. The word *situation*, however, is not because a capital *S* looks aesthetically awkward.)

With this verbal equipment I can quickly suggest that the problem of evil may be viewed in the perspective of four questions, which, consequently, constitute the parts of this book:

1. Is evil universal and, if so, why is it universal and how may it be conceived?
2. How and under what circumstances do Judges consider other persons to be Evildoers or Victims or situations to be evil-producing?
3. Why are some persons Evildoers? How can evil be prevented and combated? When is such action taken?
4. Why do some persons become Victims? How can individuals prevent themselves from becoming Victims? How can they combat the evil that befalls them?

Should animals be excluded from a discussion of evil? There is no good reason to do so from one standpoint[10] because they might be considered Evildoers (dog bites man) or Victims (man beats dog; an epidemic of rabies). In fact, animals in early Greece had to stand trial when they caused a person's death.[11] But theologians and philosophers are hard-pressed to deal with animals whenever they refer to the free will of the Evildoer. Animals, it is believed, do not "consciously" make choices between courses of action, they presumably are not aware of the consequences of what they do, and they cannot appreciate their own mortality. It is better, consequently, to relegate them to the category of any other situation when they have evil consequences for human beings or to focus upon the human Evildoer who makes them suffer or who exterminates them.

At this point a clear-cut, intelligible definition of evil is highly desirable. But where can such a definition be found? What source should one consult? Not a dictionary, because dictionaries seek only to provide common usages, with or without etymological or historical derivation. Not the Old and New Testaments of the Bible because by my count, based on a standard Concordance, the word *evil* in the King James version (or at least the translation of whatever concept may have been used in Hebrew, Greek, Latin, and other languages), is used almost 600 times.[12] The word often appears without elaboration and with so many different denotations and connotations that I do not think they can be squeezed into a tidy verbal bundle. Theology and philosophy are similarly diffuse. And the social and psychological sciences, as I have said, eschew the concept almost without exception.

Under these circumstances, I offer two criteria for establishing the existence or nonexistence of evil. One is psychological, the other social or moral: *psychological*, a condition in which one or more persons experience pain, unhappiness, frustration, or other negative, aversive feelings; *social-moral*, a condition in which aversive feelings or the actions of one or more persons are considered undesirable by one or more Judges within or outside the Victim's own society and sometimes also by the Victim or Victims themselves. Included in this criterion is a condition in which the feelings or actions of one or more persons are judged to threaten either the security or existence of the society or one or more of its basic values.

A definition of evil thus emerges; it is a state of affairs in which both of the above criteria are satisfied. Some of the crucial problems associated with defining evil seem perhaps to be avoided, but I think the definition, in spite of undefined, abstract terms, provides a setting in which these problems can be raised, dissected, and—hopefully—partially resolved. When a universal evil is identified as pain, physical pain, psychic pain, pain of all kinds, pain being endured, pain being inflicted, pain in the past, the present, and the future,[13] at first such a statement seems sensible and reminds us of Job's boils in biblical times and genocide in the modern world. The psychological criterion of pain, however, is not sufficient, for we would not call the pain evil or the dentist an Evildoer when a tooth with a cavity is being drilled. Here the social-moral criterion is unfulfilled. On the other hand, millions suffered pain and death when the Nazis deliberately killed Jews and Gentiles, when the Turks massacred Armenians during World War I, and when bombs were dropped on Dresden and Hiroshima during World War II. In these instances non-Nazi, non-Turkish, non-British, and non-American Judges would call such mass killings evil on the basis of the social-moral criterion. When it is stated in the Bible that evil refers to an individual who knows the better but follows the worse course of action, the social-moral criterion must be involved: condemnation of the failure to select what is judged to be the more desirable of two courses or departing from a central injunction of Christianity. But such a decision would not be called evil unless it can also be shown or asserted that the Evildoer is bringing evil upon Victims or himself in the short or long run or that he is victimizing himself for all eternity.

A penchant to personify evil by referring to the German Nazis has become clear even in this prologue. Should I continue to brand them as the most flagrant of Evildoers? Yes, I think so, though avenging the holocaust is not my intention. Rather I suggest that it is easy enough to demonstrate that pathological perverts may perpetrate evil, but it is much more important to say again and again that the representatives of the German people—a people capable of the greatest achievements in every field we prize, from art to science—were able to countenance perhaps the worst or nearly the worst evils imaginable and to use some of our greatest technological achievements to produce that evil. At this point, as an American, I say we are uncertain of what Americans in recent years did or planned for Europe, Cuba, Vietnam, and merely mentioning the CIA suggests that many facts remain uncertain. The whole story of Stalin in the Soviet Union is also not known. The deeds of the Nazis, however, are as well documented as Richard Nixon's deeds are substantiated by his own tapes, and they reveal the depths of evil that even the most apparently civilized, cultivated peoples tolerated or encouraged. No nation, no group, no one of us is guiltless, yet the generation of Germans in the period from 1930 to 1945, in my opinion, reached the abysmal depths of all conceivable evils. This is why they are my favored example of evil on a large scale. I am neither asking that present-day Germans be persecuted for what their elders once did nor that those elders be forgiven. The Nazis are simply a horrifying, horrible case history to serve as a warning to all mankind. The apparent ferocity of these references to them, however, should not give the impression that a main purpose of this book is to rehearse their crimes. No, evil is universal, which is the theme of the first chapter.

NOTES

1. François Petit, *The Problem of Evil* (New York: Hawthorn Books, 1959), p. 11.

2. M. B. Ahern, *The Problem of Evil* (New York: Schocken Books, 1971), p. xii.

3. Paul Weiss, "Some Neglected Ethical Questions," in Ruth Nanda Anshen, ed., *Moral Principles of Action* (New York: Harpers, 1952), pp. 207-20.

4. Robert M. MacIver, "The Deep Beauty of the Golden Rule," in Anshen, *Moral Principles,* pp. 39-47. See also Ayn Rand, *The Virtue of Selfishness* (New York: American Library, 1964), p. 4.

5. Karl E. Scheibe, "Legitimized Aggression and the Assignment of Evil," *American Scholar* 43 (1974): 576-92. Kurt H. Wolff, "For a Sociology of Evil," *Journal of Social Issues,* 25 (1969): 111-25.

6. Bernard Berelson and Gary A. Steiner, *Human Behavior* (New York: Harcourt, Brace & World, 1964), p. 712.

7. Bernard G. Rosenthal, *The Images of Man* (New York: Basic Books, 1971).

8. Richard Taylor, *Good and Evil* (New York: Macmillan, 1970), pp. 123-24.

9. Reinhold Niebuhr, *The Nature and Destiny of Man* (New York: Scribner's, 1949), p. 2.

10. Bertrand Russell, *Religion and Science* (New York: Holt, 1935), p. 203.

11. A. W. Mair, "Greek," in James Hastings, ed., *Encyclopaedia of Religion and Ethics* (New York: Scribner's, 1922), 11: 545-56.

12. James Strong, *The Exhaustive Concordance of the Bible* (New York: Abingdon-Cokesbury Press, 1890), pp. 322-23.

13. David Bakan, *Disease, Pain, Sacrifice* (Chicago: University of Chicago Press, 1968), pp. 69-71.

Part One

THE SETTING

1

UNIVERSALITY

Let there be no misunderstanding at the outset: the thesis of this chapter is that evil is universal, but few concrete details can be supplied concerning the actions or situations that are universally judged to be evil. For we are immediately faced with a perplexing problem concerning the Judge, the person who passes judgment about good and evil. The danger of ethnocentrism is great and is probably insurmountable in terms of the social-moral criterion of evil. In some societies, for example, the word for human being is the one the inhabitants use to designate themselves; by implication all outsiders are not human, are potential Evildoers. If the Judge comes from the same society as the individual or situation being judged, he may indeed apply standards comprehensible to almost everyone living in that society. If he comes from another society, however, he is likely to have a different set of values, and his judgment will be debated. Who should judge a mystical or religious ritual involving cannibalism? An outsider will be shocked; an insider may believe the ceremony essential for the functioning or survival of the society.[1] "The meaning" of the action must be understood, and "meanings are not identical with circumstances."[2] Which Judge, then, should say "evil" or "good"? And can the insider who piously praises the rite be believed? Anthropologists are "skeptical of finding behind *every* cannibal rite some moral altruism, behind every sadistic practice an offering to a—regrettably—demanding god, behind every war the feeling of a holy cause," and they consequently wonder whether "man is prone to paint himself in pleasant colors" and to be "less moral than moralizing."[3]

Even within a given society, the concept of good and evil fluctuates, for all societies are divided into social strata, variously functioning as clans, moieties, social classes, and so forth, each of which has distinctive values to maintain if its identity, power, or privileges are to be secure. Out-groupers who violate the standards, even though they are within the same society, bring pain in some form to the in-groupers and hence are branded with the epithet of evil. The concept of good and evil in any society, moreover, usually changes, if slowly, with the passing of time. O tempora, o mores—and contrast the attention paid to the problem of morality in the Middle Ages of Western civilization and the respect it commands or fails to command in the modern world.[4] *Perhaps* even during a single decade the standards of American college students shift somewhat, or at least some of them do.[5]

Under these circumstances it would be foolhardy to anticipate final solutions to any of the questions that must be raised concerning evil unless one deliberately subscribes to arbitrary standards. This is a cruel conclusion to draw, but it seems better to be blunt rather than to raise false hopes concerning eternal verities. Wild, exciting generalizations about evil cannot tolerate careful examination unless they are pitched on a very abstract level.

A generation or so ago anthropologists maintained that the search for universals is fruitless in view of the doctrine of relativity that they then extolled. Values, they proclaimed, are neither universal nor eternal; they fluctuate from society to society. If this proclamation is true, there can be no universal set of evil-arousing stimuli. Today, however, the quest for human uniformity has been renewed because it seems clear that the "same basic physiological needs" are satisfied everywhere and that each society makes provision for its "organization, operation, and perpetuation."[6] No society, for example, tolerates sexual license. Everywhere sexual intercourse between certain specified persons, particularly relatives, is taboo. Occasional violations of the taboo are permitted without being called evil, such as the requirement that royalty marry within the same immediate or extended family, but these are exceptions even within the sanctioning society. Similarly, property rights exist everywhere, although they may be loosely defined; they prescribe and proscribe appropriate behavior from which in theory no departures are permitted. Thus there are abstractions to be salvaged from relativity, but—and the *but* will be considered later on.

Intuitively, most thinking persons are convinced that, in spite of cultural variability, some kinds of situations are judged to be evil everywhere. The belief persists, although recognition is given to the fact that there are always so many different persons and situations to be judged, so many stimuli forcibly catching our attention or being pursued by us. We know that any stimulus at some time may be evaluated by someone either in terms of its effects upon individuals (the psychological criterion) or its value for others, including perhaps the persons being affected (the social-moral criterion). In fact, are stimuli always so judged? Or, if they are so judged, is the concept of evil part of the judgment?

The answer, perhaps, is *yes*. As a result of the nature of existence and the scarcity of material and symbolic goods, something always goes wrong. It is impossible not to be repeatedly reminded that perpetual bliss has never characterized mankind—truly an understatement—and that most joys are fleeting. Everywhere there is some form of "status degradation" to which someone objects or which hurts someone.[7] According to a philosopher, "Disappointed hopes, the prosperity of the wicked, the suffering of the innocent, even the little ironies of circumstance invite men to question whether the ultimate power in the universe is good or evil."[8] A theologian says, "A point on which Christian teaching is categorical" is that "evil will persist throughout eternity."[9] Or the New Testament: "For all have sinned, and come short of the glory of God."[10] A very competent humanist: "Every god has his enemy, whom he must vanquish and destroy," and "conflict between Eros and Thanatos" is truly ubiquitous.[11]

Since evaluation always requires a judgment differentiating between two kinds of values, one securing approval, the other disapproval, on this basis alone it seems reasonable to assert that evil as such is universal—but that is saying nothing more than that everywhere men judge specific persons and some situations to be evil. The assertion, however, is not without merit since at the very least it suggests man's readiness to employ the epithet. We can be certain, moreover, that the judgment will be expressed because all persons to some extent ingest and then reflect the views prevailing in their milieu. Of course, there are always rebels against the status quo in the domain of values, such as those who have the courage, originality, and ingenuity to believe that, although "this world has no ultimate meaning," still "I know that something in it has a meaning and that is man, because he is the only creature to insist on having one."[12] Such an expression is the quintessence of the humanistic position: keep searching for the difference between good and evil, do not take for granted the lessons of the ages and particularly of one's own milieu because they may be dreadfully misleading. Even those belonging to a select company, therefore, cannot perceive another person neutrally unless they force themselves to withhold judgment or unless they are able to think of him as a nonperson (like a fellow standee in a crowded bus).

Evil or the judgment of evil is perhaps universal for another reason, which is both social and semantic: every society tries to point to a sharp line between approved and disapproved values. It is easier to make a crude, black-white distinction than to recognize shades of gray. The young child who is taught the difference between good and bad, especially with reference to their real or imagined consequences, must acquire some conception of evil. To bolster the distinction, all peoples are given and then utilize stereotypes facilitating the perception of the two opposites. Information about evil, it is asserted, especially in proverbs, diffuses faster than information about good. A man's character can be destroyed more rapidly than it can be built up. Punishment to Evildoers is more painful, immediately or eventually, than the rewards from good actions. Whether such stereotypes are true is not vital; only their ubiquity and the fact that they affect Judges need be noted.

The existence of Victims is anticipated, perhaps universally, as a result of events in a mythical or historical past. In many societies, for example, people believe in a golden age that existed long ago[13]—in a Garden, elsewhere upon the earth, or in the clouds—in which mankind was innocent, not aware of evil, in a state of bliss from which human beings strayed for a reason that is symbolically represented by some concrete action or decision of theirs. As a result, their descendants carry within themselves the sins of their ancestors. With evil proneness in their heritage, they are Victims and in turn inflict evil upon others. The judgment may be made, too, from an opposite standpoint. Persons in the present are judged to be Victims becaue in the future a heavenly or utopian state of affairs is awaited in which justice triumphs and appropriate compensation is received.

In proclaiming the universality of evil in the abstract, we are in effect saying that human beings are universally Evildoers and Victims. Only a few slightly puzzling instances require brief explanations to substantiate this generalization. First are situations: it is individuals who either produce or are affected by the situations judged to be evil. A dark

cloud in the sky may foreshadow a tornado; presumably not a consequence of human action, it is judged to be potentially good or evil only
in terms of its assumed consequences upon persons. If it results in rain
falling upon parched farmland, it might be called good; if it produces
hurricane-force winds that destroy property and cause death, it certainly would be called evil; if it merely causes some persons to cancel a
picnic, the judgment would be mild. A human being passes the judgment; without him, I say again, there is no good or evil. A Judge passes
judgment, in this and in all other instances, whenever he finds or
thinks there will be Victims. Sometimes—and war is a first-rate illustration—the Judge may locate not only the Victims but also the persons he believes to be Evildoers. Some situations are so perfectly correlated with human misery that they can be called evil, almost whether
the social-moral criterion for evil is satisfied and even when we may not
be able to identify the Evildoers. Can we name all the Evildoers who in
the past have generated hatred between two countries? I doubt it, although of course some can be located; we know with certainty only that
present generations have inherited and perpetuate what their ancestors
once began either deliberately or in a sporadic fashion, whether or not
they are now justified in doing so.

Any person above the level of an idiot passes judgment on himself at
some time and finds that self deficient with respect to some standard
prevailing within his society or within himself. Though systematic
evidence is lacking, I think we have here another reason to strengthen
our faith in the universality of evil. The self-judgments obviously involve a single human being who is both Judge and, depending on his
judgment, a Victim or an Evildoer. In retrospect, a saint may judge
himself to have been an Evildoer during his oat-sowing days and subsequently to have become a Victim of that mode of living. In still other
cases, an outside Judge believes that the Evildoer and the Victim are the
same person; a suicide is thus branded by a Judge considering self-
destruction a sin and hence evil. This reference to suicide compels us to
peer at the problem of responsibility: Is the suicide really responsible
for his act? Have not other persons driven him to the desperate decision?
Are not they the real Evildoers? We may never know.

Doubtless like the reader I myself grow impatient as these abstractions
flit by. Is it possible to be more specific concerning the universality of
evil? Consider incest; whoever commits incest in any society is judged

an Evildoer. It is simple enough to say more concretely that this taboo involves sexual relations between very close relatives, such as father and daughter or mother and son. The statement, however, fails to indicate whether intercourse or marriage between other relatives, such as cross- and and parallel-cousins, is encouraged or prohibited in a particular society. Variability with respect to these other relatives is great, and hence this particular evil cannot be delineated in detail. The closest research has come in determining the conditions affecting the definition of incest is one study in which it appears that *perhaps* the residence of the newly married pair tends to determine the name given various kin, and the name in turn tends to influence the relatives considered taboo.[14] But there are exceptions to such correlational associations; hence we cannot be certain that residence can enable us to anticipate which persons in a given society are considered taboo breakers and hence evil, although the inhabitants themselves have quite adequate knowledge on that score.

The search for specific evils is no more successful when attention is focused upon good or the opposite of evil. This could be a legitimate procedure because it is difficult (if not impossible) to conceive of one without the other, although St. Augustine maintained that good can exist without evil, just as there can be a vase without a crack but no crack without a vase.[15] Immediately we must note that an expert who is supposed to command knowledge concerning the problem of good answers his own question, "Is there a single property by virtue of which all intrinsic or inherent goods are good?" by stating that "this question has often been answered affirmatively, but none of the affirmative answers has met with general favor."[16] A philosopher may offer assurance that surely there are certain "ultimate and objective" values such as truth, goodness, beauty, and happiness that must be related to the problem of good and evil.[17] But what do these abstract concepts mean in reality? "Beauty," yes, but what happens when we employ the word to describe a Gothic cathedral or a modern building of reinforced cement? Does assent mean anything more than verbal nodding? I feel equally critical and skeptical when someone in good faith tries to indicate the dominant values of any country, such as the United States: "The survival of the society, the welfare of the society, the advancement of the society, and the reality-adjustment of the society."[18] The glib phrases sound valid, at least until one tries to imagine a country they do not describe equally well.

Surely we ought to be able to rescue ourselves from this discouraging state of affairs. There must be some way to extract out of the codes of mankind, such as the Ten Commandments in the Judeo-Christian tradition or the standards of conduct considered ideal by traditional Zulus, various hints concerning the evils securing more or less universal designation as a result of the trials and errors of all mankind. Both brave and reckless thinkers have attempted to extract such a list on the basis of their own experience, intuition, prejudices, and hunches—but no one of them has surveyed all the evidence because our knowledge is inadequate and also because nobody appears to have had the wisdom enabling him to reduce staggering heterogeneity to a valid but inclusive formulation in the manner of an Einstein. Here is a sample of the generalizations (or perhaps they should be called platitudes):

EVIL

"disease and death"[19]
"things fade" and "alternatives exclude"[20]
"sickness, accident, death, penury, destructive forces of nature"[21]
"anything that we all dread"[22]
"contrary" of "justice, gratitude, modesty, equity, mercy, and the rest of the laws of nature"[23]
"bad seasons and bad markets"[24]
"the beggars, the terrible poverty, the prevalence of disease, the anarchy and corruption in politics"[25]
"war"[26]
that which "works out badly, frustrating men's endeavors."[27]

GOOD

"purpose" in "life"; rationality of "man"; "supreme importance" of "the individual"; importance of "material progress"; "certain basic social institutions"; and "other miscellaneous beliefs and attitudes"[28]
"a reverence for life"[29]
"security"[30]
"a pool of meaning drawing across generations and solidly between individuals"; "the daily celebration of life"; "a rich participation in a broad panorama of life experiences"; "self-feeling"[31]
"act spontaneously"; "relate to the other as a whole, indeterminate individual"; "grant another the right to his own center"[32]

"the internal satisfaction of our minds, the external advantages of our
body, and the enjoyment of such possessions as we have acquired
by our industry and good fortune"[33]
"reciprocity"[34]
"morality" and "self-interest"[35]
"being a good mother," "prohibition against incest," "control of
in-group aggression," "distributive justice"[36]
"fundamental human rights," "dignity and worth of the human
person," "the equal rights of men and women and of nations large
and small," "social progress and better standards of life in larger
freedom"[37]

A longer inventory could be collected, but it would contribute little
to what seem to be two consequences. First, many conceptions of evil
utilize the psychological criterion. Unquestionably, death and disease,
for example, are to be avoided under all circumstances; it is painful to
have "things fade" or to be unable to choose one alternative rather than
another. On the other hand, the social-moral criteria involved in the
conceptualizations of the good cannot easily be reduced to a simple
formulation merely by considering their antonyms as evil. Some have
psychological consequences; the absence of security is painful, as is the
inability to enjoy one's own possessions. Most of the values, however,
involve social relations, the effect one person has upon another who
would seem to be the potential or the actual Victim. There are scarcities
inherent in any society relating to food, compatible or incompatible
sexual partners, honors, and statuses, all of which involve to some extent
friction in interpersonal relations. The verbal expression varies, but
some form of reciprocation always seems to be implied. We have here,
then, at least the glimpse of a foundation on which to build.

To be sure, it is possible to criticize the social-moral criteria as being
ethnocentric, for all of them have been formulated by Western men and
reflect their traditions. "Life has purpose" is an example. Not every
person in every society would agree that denying a purpose to existence
is necessarily evil; an agnostic might claim that perhaps it has purpose,
perhaps not. "Material progress is important": surely that is an ethnocentric value, if ever there be one. "Reverence for life" seems glorious
until one tries to see its practical implication; was the particular formu-

lator of that value really showing reverence for life when in reality he tended to treat his African patients reverentially but like children?

Perhaps there is a semblance of cross-cultural uniformity in connection with some situations. Earthquakes are probably condemned by everyone, except by those interpreting them as an expression of a deity's design. Even on a psychological level, however, the uniformity appears elusive the moment one concentrates upon specific causal sequences. In the 1960s, for example, samples of adults in a dozen countries were asked a very straightforward question: "What are your fears and worries about the future?" Assume that "fears and worries" are symptomatic of or related to evil in some form; then we immediately note great variability from country to country. Thus 82 percent of the sample in the Dominican Republic mentioned economic matters and only 30 percent in Brazil.[38] If we push aside skepticism concerning the validity of such replies, it is necessary to ask whether "fears and worries" had the same meaning in these two countries. The same figures also indicate, once again, variability within each society, even as within a culture optimists use the words *good* and *just* more frequently than do pessimists.

We have thus both universality and variability: universality on a very abstract level, variability with reference to the application within specific societies. The universality suggests the common though uncertain denominators on which men everywhere agree and provide hope, however faint, for understanding and even eradicating some of the evil that plagues us. Great men can then arise from time to time and enable their followers to secure new insights into existence and thus perhaps fortify them to battle what they judge to be evil.[39] In the West the view persists that in Eden man fell from an original state of perfection, and he has been and forever will be in a state of sin from which he tries to recover during his mortal existence. A theologian advancing a contrary view— that man has been evolving and now finally has achieved a conscience enabling him to choose between good and evil—may not be heard at first as a result of the ancient, sustained tradition perpetuated by a holy Bible.[40] For this reason, perhaps most theologians continue to maintain that evil violates an established or preordained relation between the Evildoer and his God and that immediately or eventually he will suffer. This chapter, therefore, ends on the same unsatisfactory note with which it began: there are vague universals, but they vary. Perhaps the universals provide at least a challenge, and the variations the hope and the possibility of change. At any rate, both the universals and the variations stem from the complexities about to be considered.

NOTES

1. Garry Hogg, *Cannibalism and Human Sacrifice* (London: Robert Hale, 1958), p. 17.

2. Karl Duncker, "Ethical Relativity?" *Mind* 48 (1939): 39-57.

3. May Edel and Abraham Edel, *Anthropology and Ethics* (Cleveland: Case Western Reserve University, 1968), p. 29.

4. Ernest Becker, *The Structure of Evil* (New York: George Braziller, 1968), pp. 16-17.

5. For example, Paul Crissman, "Temporal Change and Sexual Difference in Moral Judgment," *Journal of Social Psychology* 16 (1942): 29-38.

6. Ralph Linton, "Universal Ethical Principles: An Anthropological View," in Ruth Nanda Anshen, ed., *Moral Principles of Action* (New York: Harpers, 1952), pp. 645-60.

7. Harold Garfinkel, "Conditions of Successful Degradation Ceremonies," *American Journal of Sociology*, 61 (1956): 420-24.

8. William Chase Greene, *Moira: Fate, Good, and Evil in Greek Thought* (Cambridge: Harvard University Press, 1944), p. 5.

9. François Petit, *The Problem of Evil* (New York: Hawthorn Books, 1959), p. 125.

10. Rom. 3:23.

11. Joseph Fontenrose, *Python* (Berkeley: University of California Press, 1959), pp. 1, 474.

12. Albert Camus, *Resistance, Rebellion, and Death* (New York: Knopf, 1961), p. 28.

13. Cf. Greene, *Moira.*

14. George Peter Murdock, *Social Structure* (New York: Macmillan, 1949), pp. 148, 287-88.

15. Richard Cavendish, *The Powers of Evil* (New York: Putnam's, 1975), p. 6.

16. Robert G. Olson, "The Good," in Paul Edwards, ed., *Encyclopedia of Philosophy* (New York: Macmillan, 1967), 3: 367-70. See also W. D. Niven, "Good and Evil," in James Hastings, ed., *Encyclopaedia of Religion and Ethics* (New York: Scribner's, 1922), 6: 318-26.

17. C. E. M. Joad, *Guide to Modern Wickedness* (London: Faber and Faber, 1939), p. 15.

18. Nicholas Rescher, "The Study of Value Change," in Ervin Laszlo and James B. Wilbur, eds., *Value Theory in Philosophy and Social Science* (New York: Gordon and Breach, 1973), pp. 12-23.

19. Ernest Becker, *Escape from Evil* (New York: Free Press, 1975), p. 2.

20. Alfred N. Whitehead, cited by Becker, *Structure of Evil*, p. 379.

21. Niven, "Good and Evil," p. 318.

22. Bertrand Russell, *Religion and Science* (New York: Holt, 1935), p. 242.

23. Thomas Hobbes, *Leviathan*, in Frederick A. Olafson, ed., *Society, Law, and Morality* (Englewood Cliffs: Prentice-Hall, 1961), p. 90.

24. G. E. Fussell, cited by *Webster's Third International Dictionary* (Springfield: Merriam, 1963), p. 789.

25. Bertrand Russell, cited by ibid.

26. *Charter of the United Nations.*

27. Richard Taylor, *Good and Evil* (New York: Macmillan, 1970), p. 38.

28. Gail M. Inlow, *Values in Transition* (New York: Wiley, 1972), p. 21.

29. Albert Schweitzer, "He That Loses His Life Shall Find It," in Anshen, *Moral Principles*, pp. 673-91.

30. John David Garcia, *The Moral Society* (New York: Julian Press, 1971), p. 24.

31. Becker, *Structure of Evil*, pp. 229, 230, 247, 328.

32. Martin Buber, cited in ibid., p. 272.

33. David Hume," A Treatise of Human Nature," in Olafson, *Society*, p. 310.

34. Alvin W. Gouldner, "The Norm of Reciprocity," *American Sociological Review* 25 (1960): 161-78.

35. Kurt Baier, *The Moral Point of View* (Ithaca: Cornell University Press, 1958), p. 187.

36. Edel and Edel, *Anthropology*, pp. 36, 42, 44, 53, 68.

37. *Charter of the United Natons.*

38. Hadley Cantril, *The Pattern of Human Concerns* (New Brunswick: Rutgers University Press, 1965), p. 170.

39. Cf. Becker, *Structure of Evil*, p. 64.

40. Mary Frances Thelen, introduction to F. R. Tennant, *The Sources of the Doctrines of the Fall and Original Sin* (New York: Schocken Books, 1968), p. ii.

2

BASES

Evil is universal as a result of the nature of man and his society and also of an inevitable system of theology to which he subscribes. Although human beings differ with respect to their appearance and individuality, their talents and capabilities, they also share many reactions and a common destiny. The shared reactions include the ones specified by the psychological criterion of evil: the capacity to experience pain and then to try to avoid or mitigate it. No matter where he lives, any individual is likely to flinch when his skin is pierced without benefit of anaesthetic.

Almost no one, I think, who has ever speculated concerning man's destiny has failed to be aware of his own mortality as a result of illness, accidents, legal or illegal murder, and age.[1] Animals struggle to survive, but presumably they are not conscious of their inevitable doom. For human beings, the fear of death is probably universal at some time and is likely to be accompanied by psychic pain. Fatalism, according to one historian of religion, is "probably rooted psychologically in the fact of evil and the inevitability of death."[2] Certainly the painful anticipation of death meets the psychological criterion of evil and probably satisfies the social-moral criterion too; with important exceptions (when abortion or euthanasia is considered), death itself violates a basic value, the will to live. The fact that human adults are universally conscious of their mortality, however, provides no sound reason to trace all evil to this one source. Crimes of passion seem far removed from such an awareness unless the language is strained to the point of maintaining that this form of evildoing must ultimately be motivated by a desire to dominate and hence achieve a kind of immortality, but this interpretation seems psychologically far-fetched. The leaders behind imperialism or colonization may be motivated to perpetuate their names and thus symbolically circumvent death, but such reductionism overlooks more tangible gains that are sought and that pertain to the here-and-now.

It is not pain or suffering per se, I repeat, that is evil or judged evil. Clearly there are noxious stimuli everywhere that produce pain and suffering or noxious reactions. These stimuli may provide universal bases as a component of evil, but their universality satisfies only the psychological criterion, not the social-moral one. Although childbirth is almost always painful, only a real misogynist would consider it evil.

The natural environment into which all men are plunged has its limitations. The inhabitants in a benign climate, where food is plentiful and weather predictable, have a different concept of evil from those living in a harsh environment where it is difficult to eke out an existence. But an attitude toward evil has cultural components not directly derivable from nature, yet definitely affecting judgments. Navaho Indians, for example, while they may seek to influence nature through ritual and song as well as through actions, by and large accept natural forces and try to adapt themselves to them. "If a flood comes and washes out a formerly fertile village, one does not try to dam the stream and replace the soil; instead one moves to a floodless spot."[3] For Navaho Judges, therefore, nature exists and its effects are less likely to be judged evil, though with an attitude of resignation they must feel, at a very minimum, disturbed when compelled to move on. The natural situation, in short, is likely to produce some pain or trouble.

Everyone at some time fails to achieve a goal as a result of natural situations or other human beings and hence inevitably is frustrated. The frustration itself is painful and, whether significant or trivial, is likely to elicit aggression. To avoid the quibbling characterizing modern analyses of frustration and aggression, I emphasize that the frustrated person is likely to be aggressive, but it is not absolutely certain that he will be. Being aggressive may mean that actually or in fantasy, intentionally or unintentionally, he would hurt some person or persons (or their surrogate),[4] and thus in some sense he is responsible for one or more Victims. "No society," an anthropologist has observed in a double negative that makes him sound omniscient, "has successfully solved the problem of preventing psychic aggression" and hence "no society on record . . . does not have an ethical system."[5] Transgressing an ethical system in turn is judged immoral and hence, according to social-moral criteria, is evil. If it is true that "a norm of reciprocity" is universal ("people should help those who have helped them, and . . . should not injure those who have helped them"),[6] then the violation of the norm is likely to be considered frustrating, and certainly violations are everywhere to be anticipated.

To attempt to list the various and numerous frustrations to which human beings are doomed is plainly impossible. Two totally different sources may serve as illustrations. Socialization, in spite of the mythology of the "happy childhood," is never a completely gratifying experience. Parents are imperfect; however great their love and however noble their intentions, they make mistakes from the child's viewpoint. Second, contact with the West has frustrated many or most persons in developing societies when their freedom has been abridged and their cultures changed significantly as a result of formal or informal (that is, economic or cultural) colonization.[7]

Since natural limitations and human interactions produce frustrations and the probability of aggression, every society evolves what outsiders call an ethical system and what the individuals themselves recognize as compulsions and taboos. Human beings cannot develop and live together without rules and regulations they consider good and hence that lead to approved goals and away from disapproved ones. Violations are taboo.[8] I shall use the concept in its modern English spelling; "tabu" in the original Polynesian sense refers to an object or person either feared or considered otherwise mysterious and hence unsafe for human contact. A "tabu" on touching the skirt of a powerful king or having intercourse with a menstruating woman may seem more significant than a legally formulated "taboo" on driving in the wrong direction on a one-way street or picking wild flowers on an Alpine peak, but in all these instances a human being makes a judgment concerning prohibited behavior. For all I know, driving down a one-way street in the old days in Zanzibar when the sultan was approaching in his flaming red car was more of a crime (or considered a greater sin) than touching his skirt. A single word can serve to designate the rule, the regulation, the ordinance, the law, the etiquette that is not supposed to be violated—and "taboo" seems admirably suitable for that purpose. From yet another standpoint the concept of taboo is useful because it may refer not only to shared behavior but also to idiosyncratic actions. Freud believed he had discovered striking parallels between the taboos of what his generation called "savages" and the behavior of neurotics in Austrian society; he reported that other psychoanalysts had "come across people who have created for themselves individual taboo prohibitions of this very kind and who obey them just as strictly as savages obey the communal taboos of their tribe or society."[9]

Taboos exist everywhere, therefore, because human beings live with one another, and hence their impulses must be curbed.[10] They are thus like plants and animals whose freedom to grow, produce, and reproduce is limited by the surrounding milieu. But only human beings are aware of limitations; hence they try to verbalize and justify them in terms of some explicit code or philosophy containing criteria for evil. You know what you are supposed to do; you are deliberately taught the moral rules of your society; you are aware of transgressions because you are shocked by them. Innocent children gradually learn the boundaries they should not cross. Only those unable to participate fully in society because their brains are too severely damaged or because they are so psychotic that presumably they lack adequate contact with reality are excluded from the process of complete indoctrination.

Taboos are also believed to be useful and helpful: "They tend to preserve the past and to control the impingement of the future on the present."[11] They point out the dangers persons in a society must avoid if they are to remain within its fold and to be considered respectable.[12] The presence of taboos also serves the double function of providing social sanctions and provoking fear among actual or potential Evildoers.[13] Whether they do alleviate anxiety rather than create it is a moot question. They probably do both by indicating what and where the forbidden fruits are. In the absence of "legitimated social control and arrangements," many of which involve taboos, evil in important human interactions may be ascribed to those Evildoers who are called witches or said to possess "evil eyes."[14] "Magic," it is further suggested, "is invariably associated with taboos,"[15] presumably among traditional peoples or, from time to time, among even the most sophisticated Westerners.

The taboos of a society are not necessarily formulated through formal legislation. Perhaps they are deduced from some valued source such as the Bible. They may be arrived at pragmatically: the good values the taboos would protect are those that work, are efficient, or seem beneficial. Outsiders may consider them Hegelian in the sense of being predetermined by history.[16]

Evil, explicitly or implicitly, is likely to be a central motif within not only a society's ethical system but also its proverbs, folktales, poetry, and literature.[17] These forms of expression, it might be argued from a Marxian viewpoint, are the superstructure of the society and are truly inescapable. In our society, fairy tales are said to be enjoyed by children because they offer a simple, straightforward dichotomy between good and evil through their characters who symbolize either one but not both of the two extremes and with whom identification is easy and intelligible. According to the stories, "Evil is not without its attractions—symbolized by the might of the giant or dragon, the power of the witch, the cunning of the queen in 'Snow White'—and often it is temporarily in the ascendancy."

The reference to fairy tales raises the much more general problem of how the taboos and values of a society are ascertained. In our own society we know there is no easy route to such knowledge. Our proverbs tell us that a penny saved is a penny gained and also to enjoy ourselves now because tomorrow we die. Which proverb has greater influence? The contradictions reflect different values at the moment or in the past. To try to ascertain current views more accurately, social scientists and those engaged in market research rely heavily upon polls and surveys because the results are or can be based upon truly random samples and because the procedures are neatly standardized. The fact that polls in Western countries are almost always able to forecast the outcome of an election does not mean that they have universal validity for all topics that might be investigated. Even when these considerations are waived, the problem of modal values is not always solved since people, like their proverbs and biblical injunctions, seldom reach unanimity. Anthropologists often worry less about formal schedules and more about the rapport they establish with their informants by living in the society and perhaps learning its language; and through participant observation they seek clues to subtle values. One sociologist has suggested that other methods besides these formal ones and in addition to the content analyses of folktales might provide insights into the nature of what is considered evildoing in a given society: the ordeals that are practiced, the imagery that appears in dreams, the content of the formal educational system, and the prevailing techniques of censorship.[18]

The institution par excellence that concerns itself with evil, aside from government, is religion. For most religions, certainly for those with clearly formulated theologies, the existence of evil is a necessity. In the West this necessity is linked to freedom: evil occurs when the individual knows the difference between right and wrong and nevertheless chooses the wrong course of action. Just as economists postulate an Economic Man who is able to make rational decisions concerning economic matters, so theologians assume a Theologic Man capable of making right rather than wrong decisions. (Reference, consequently, will be made to Theologic Man from time to time throughout this analysis.)

The wrong course of action that is chosen involves the breaking of a taboo, and the society or its priests stand ready to disapprove. The disapproval is expressed by the threat or actuality of earthly punishment or eventual divine retribution. Again, of course, there is variability. Some societies cultivate guilt, others shame, when codes are violated. "For us, to act as we want to act necessarily involves freedom of choice," but for members of other societies "the concept is meaningless."[19] The fact that there *may* be some relation between the structure of religion and the society's own social structure[20] provides yet another reason to question the extent to which specific values can be universal over and above environmental and social conditions. In any case, it is essential to repeat that whatever imperative the society stresses is learned during socialization and that normal human beings have this capability.

Cassandra, who speaks to all of us, says we are doomed. On an actuarial basis we know that evil has always existed and persisted. On an analytic basis we now also know that the bases for evil are inherent in man, his environment, and the society he creates. There is no escape from evil; we are accursed, she repeats. Mitigate, combat, prevent some evil, yes— but abolish altogether? No, no, at least not until the millennium is reached. But the millennium may be followed by another Garden, which will most certainly contain a serpent and a tree.

NOTES

1. Richard Cavendish, *The Powers of Evil* (New York: Putnam's, 1975), p. 33.

2. A. Eustace Haydon, "Fatalism," in Edwin R. A. Seligman, ed., *Encyclopaedia of the Social Sciences* (New York: Macmillan, 1930), 6: 146-48.

3. Clyde and Dorothea Kluckhohn, *The Navaho* (Cambridge: Harvard University Press, 1946), p. 227.

4. Arnold H. Buss, "Aggression Pays," in Jerome L. Singer, ed., *The Control of Aggression and Violence* (New York: Academic Press, 1971), pp. 7-18.

5. Ralph Linton, "Universal Ethical Principles," in Ruth Nanda Anshen, ed., *Moral Principles of Action* (New York: Harpers, 1952), pp. 645-60.

6. Alvin W. Gouldner, "The Norm of Reciprocity," *American Sociological Review* 25 (1960): 161-78.

7. Thomas Hodgkin, "The Idea of Freedom in African National Movements," in David Bidney, ed., *The Concept of Freedom in Anthropology* (Hague: Mouton, 1963), pp. 208-27.

8. June L. Tapp and Lawrence Kohlberg, "Developing Senses of Law and Legal Justice," *Journal of Social Issues* 27, no. 2 (1971): 65-71.

9. Sigmund Freud, *Totem and Taboo* (New York: W. W. Norton, 1950), p. 26.

10. Kurt Von Fritz, "Relative and Absolute Values," in Anshen, *Moral Principles*, pp. 94-121.

11. Norman L. Farberow, *Taboo Topics* (New York: Atherton Press, 1963), p. 2.

12. Franz Steiner, *Taboo* (Baltimore: Penguin Books, 1967).

13. A. R. Radcliffe-Brown, *Taboo* (Cambridge: Cambridge University Press, 1939), p. 39.

14. Guy E. Swanson, *The Birth of the Gods* (Ann Arbor: University of Michigan Press, 1960), p. 151.

15. Farberow, *Taboo Topics*, p. 6.

16. Gail M. Inlow, *Values in Transition* (New York: Wiley, 1972), pp. 4-5.

17. Bruno Bettelheim, *The Uses of Enchantment* (New York: Knopf, 1976). See also Marie-Louise von Franz, "The Problem of Evil in Fairy Tales," Curatorium of the C. G. Jung Institute, *Evil*. (Evanston: Northwestern University Press, 1967), pp. 83-119.

18. Kurt H. Wolff, "For a Sociology of Evil," *Journal of Social Issues* 25, no. 1 (1969): 111-25.

19. Dorothy Lee, *Freedom and Culture* (Englewood Cliffs: Prentice-Hall 1959), p. 102.

20. Swanson, *Birth of the Gods*.

3

SANCTIONS

If evildoing is universal, the sanctions to prevent or discourage its appearance must also be universal. For by definition potential Victims and the society as a whole would avoid the pain of evil or the violation of prevailing social-moral codes. The principal, universal sanction against evil is punishment, the forms of which are most varied, ranging from public disapproval to decapitation, from statements of regret to violent retaliation, from avid publicity to careful secrecy. Many of the external punishments are inflicted by the Evildoer's own peers. He loses their love; he is hated by them for the havoc he has wrought. Evil will out, it is commonly believed; the Evildoer's identity eventually is known, and social disapproval is then expressed. The Victim complains or the Evildoer himself eventually acknowledges his guilt. The stereotype of the weeping, contrite, prostrate Evildoer may also have some basis in reality. It is difficult to be disloyal to one's family, peer group, or nation without feeling some trace of guilt.

A special form of sanction involves punishing those who fail to punish Evildoers. In some societies prestige is lost and the individual is probably branded a coward or a weakling who shrinks from his duty when he does not return from battle with the Evildoer's head or other parts of his body, literally or symbolically. The retaliation, however, must be carried out in a socially approved manner. In our society, political leaders who do not remove Evildoers from public office or prosecutors who do not apprehend them are believed to be corrupt and punishable, at least on a verbal level.

The sanctions against evil are accompanied by explanations, more often than not provided by the society or, rather, by the leaders of institutions within the society. Reasons for refraining from evildoing are first introduced to children as they are socialized, and thereafter they are repeated either formally by religious and political leaders or informally by word of mouth or through public censure. To a major or minor degree, the explanations perforce reflect the moral, political, and scientific view prevailing within the society or group to which the Judge, the Evildoer, or the Victim belongs.

When we inquire concerning an explanation for the existence of these explanations, we are tritely but cogently reminded that the human being "is less driven by adrenalin than he is drugged by symbols, by cultural belief systems, by abstractions like flags and anthems."[1] More concretely, the explanations serve three different functions: they justify the taboos and hence the need to avoid evildoing; they provide reasons for the fact that evil persists in spite of the penalties that are incurred for violating the taboos; and they induce individuals to become or remain Evildoers by suggesting that the evil is not evil.

Examples of each category are close at hand. Taboo'd foods, it is said, must be avoided because they are unclean or because avoiding them reminds members of their loyalty to a group whose rules of all kinds, including dietary ones, are to be followed if overall evil is to be sidestepped and, perhaps, if salvation is to be attained. More generally, pollution, whether personal or societal, is condemned, and the reasons range from health to religion.

For the second category—explaining the presence of evil—we turn first to the basic assumption behind Theologic Man: even among non-Christians, the view prevails that we have eaten of the Tree that brings us a knowledge of good and evil, and this knowledge of both alternatives cannot be repressed. In actual fact, the basic causes for evil situations are likely to be complex and may lie buried in a thousand and one factors both past and present. The prevailing explanation, however, is likely to be simple and consequently intelligible. Poverty, for example, has innumerable antecedents, but most Judges who experience or perceive this particular evil situation are likely to provide themselves with some simple rationale to account for its origin and persistence: it's their own fault, capitalism is to blame, that is their *karma*, it is God's will, their birthrate is too high.

Sanctions for a special form of evil, "undeserved suffering," are also essential since every man, at some point in his existence, feels that the pain he endures or sees others enduring is either unnecessary or fortuitous.[2] The myths of a society serve this function, for they attempt to account not only for the origin of mankind and for the changes throughout history in the past but also for evil and sin.[3] All religions seek to explain the existence of such evil, whether they call it an illusion (for example, the Vendata teachings of Hinduism), a result of a dualism reflecting opposing deities (ancient Zoroastrianism), or a combination of God's will and man's fraility, which means "an attempt to reconcile the unlimited goodness of an all-powerful God with the reality of evil" (Christianity).[4] A philosophy of evil, whether derived from myths, religions, or experience, may not be deliberately formulated with the skill and sophistication of a professional philosopher or theologian, but it helps make existence more tolerable.

The third category—the encouragement of actions that are considered evil by some Judges and perhaps under ordinary circumstances by the Evildoer himself—involves a release from existing taboos. One kills twins at birth if they symbolize evil. Enemy cities are bombed in self-defense. In Nazi Germany, "The destruction of the Jews was represented as a 'hygienic' process against 'Jewish vermin.' "[5] Similarly, many individuals are not cruel because they receive sadistic or pathological satisfaction from evildoing but because they have been taught and hence feel they are carrying out the Lord's work or otherwise are somehow contributing to the common good.

Explanations as rationalizations prevail especially in connection with prejudice against other perceivable groups, the result of which is often the evil of discrimination or war.[6] Then the prejudiced do not experience a discrepancy between their prejudice and their ideals or other values; according to a cliche' of the professionals, dissonance is reduced. A difficulty, even the most violent critics against bigotry admit, is that there is always some grain of truth in prejudice, the truth to be found either in the persons against whom the prejudice is expressed or in the fantasies of those subscribing to its directive. It is, moreover, so easy either to rationalize a justification or to ignore a contradiction between a conception of the good and a contemplated evil. A philosopher maintains:

. . . enthusiastic Nazis seem to have believed that it was their duty to do things which we are convinced are completely wrong, such as ill-treating the Jews; but is there any reason to think these Nazis really wanted to arrive at the truth regarding the question whether it was right or wrong to send Jews to concentration camps? If not, we need not be so surprised that they did not attain the truth they did not seek.[7]

The codes of a society and the sanctions they indicate or imply are not always clear or consistent. This conclusion emerges, I think, whenever the world's religious or important ethical systems are contemplated. In a treatise on *I Ching*'s Immutable Law of Change, for example, it is contended that "could we but analyze the pattern of changes governed by this Law and could we but relate our affairs to the right point in the everlasting process of ebb and flow, increase and decrease, rising and falling we should be able to determine the best action to be taken in each case." But when Theologic Man looks to this source for specific advice, he is offered what appears to be a flat banality: "To my mind, what distinguishes a Superior Man more than any other ornament of character is that he is one who knows WHEN NOT TO ACT."[8] Of course, principles distinguishing good from evil, as one good priest expressed himself to me, pervade both the Old and the New Testament like an unbroken thread. I have already said that the almost six hundred references to the word *evil* in the Scriptures cannot be neatly summarized. Here I would emphasize that contention by quoting from a standard dictionary of the Bible, which states that the concept of evil "is not easily made precise in Biblical thought, for it is hard to distinguish between what we would call sin on the one hand and what we would call disaster on the other."[9] To indicate the difficulty, following are the first three and the last three citations that appear in a long list under the rubric "evil" in *The Home Book of Bible Quotations*:[10]

. . . the imagination of man's heart is evil from his youth. . . .[11]

Because sentence against an evil work is not executed speedily, therefore the heart of the sons of men is fully set in them to do evil.[12]

. . . the heart of the sons of men is full of evil, and madness is in their hearts while they live, and after that they go to the dead.[13]

. . . But if thou do that which is evil, be afraid; for he beareth not the sword in vain; for he is the minister of God, a revenger to execute wrath upon him that doeth evil.[14]

Beloved, follow not that which is evil, but that which is good. He that doeth good is of God; but he that doeth evil hath not seen God.[15]

Let love be without dissimulation. Abhor that which is evil; cleave to that which is good.[16]

Again it is not easy to uncover the code that should be the guide to conduct in those six passages; perhaps the conflict or the problem has been stated most unequivocally by Jesus Himself:

Ye have heard that it has been said, An eye for an eye, and a tooth for a tooth: But I say unto you, That ye resist not evil; but whosoever shall smite thee on thy right cheek, turn to him the other also. And if any man will sue thee at the law, and take away thy coat, let him have thy cloak also.[17]

Even a casual reading of these injunctions suggests a truism: any taboo against evil implies approval of the opposite course of action, which therefore is judged to be good. Positive rather than negative sanctions provide rewards. The rewards for not engaging in evil behavior are numerous; they involve not only survival but also the prestige that comes from conformity and status. The universal problem, unsolved in our time, is to have the rewards of approved or good behavior outweigh those from disapproved or bad behavior, or to have the nonrewards of the former be less than the punishments associated with the latter.

The decision to apply sanctions against Evildoers (or, for that matter, to render aid to Victims) will be more relevantly discussed in the two chapters of this book devoted to combating evil. But I would note here in passing that the use of sanctions is like the administration of justice in a Western law court: because extenuating circumstances of a psychological nature may be taken into account, they are not automatically invoked. The extenuating circumstances may have a historical foundation. One writer believes that "the burning problem of good and evil was remote from most people's lives" when Hiroshima was bombed in 1945.[18] I would add, it must have been remote for the decision to have been made and then tolerated. There is, in brief, a distinction between the theoretical and the actual force of existing sanctions.

An appropriate conclusion for this part on the setting of evil is to suggest once more that evil, though its precise forms vary, exists or is thought to exist universally and that Judges possess norms to which they conform or do not conform and which they believe justify or do not justify the behavior they judge to be good or evil. Mankind may always have to choose between freedom and security,[19] Cassandra speaks up again, and involved in the choice is some concept of evil. Like it or not, this seems to be our universal destiny.

NOTES

1. Arthur Koestler, cited by Ernest Becker, *Escape from Evil* (New York: Free Press, 1975), p. 134.

2. Richard Cavendish, *The Powers of Evil* (New York: Putnam's, 1975), pp. 1, 5.

3. Paul Ricoeur, *The Symbolism of Evil* (New York: Harper & Row, 1967), pp. 162-63.

4. John Hick, "The Problem of Evil," in Paul Edwards, ed., *The Encyclopedia of Philosophy* (New York: Macmillan, 1967), 3: 136-41.

5. Stanley Milgram, *Obedience to Authority* (New York: Harper & Row, 1974), p. 186.

6. Becker, *Escape from Evil*, p. 98.

7. A. C. Ewing, *The Definition of Good* (New York: Macmillan, 1947), p. 22.

8. John Blofeld, *I Ching* (New York: Dutton, 1968), pp. 9, 42.

9. James Hastings, *Dictionary of the Bible* (New York: Scribner's, 1963), p. 277.

10. Burton Stevenson, *The Home Book of Bible Quotations* (New York: Harpers, 1949).

11. Gen. 8:21.

12. Eccles. 8:11.

13. Ibid. 9:3.

14. Rom. 13:4.

15. 3 John 1:11.

16. Rom. 12:9.

17. Matt. 5:38-40.

18. Ernest Becker, *The Structure of Evil* (New York: George Braziller, 1968), p. 17.

19. David Bidney, "The Varieties of Human Freedom," in David Bidney, ed., *The Concept of Freedom in Anthropology* (Hague: Mouton, 1963), pp. 11-34.

Part Two

JUDGMENTS

4

STIMULI AND PERCEPTION

We now seek to comprehend how and why one or more individuals are judged to be Evildoers or Victims and some situations are thought to be evil. Each Judge cannot be considered in the abstract as his judgment is analyzed, for it depends upon whether he is perceiving a peer or a stranger and upon whether he is a child or an adult, an employer or an employee, a scientist or a poet. There is always an interaction between him and the person, persons, or situation being judged. If someone deliberately kills a very young infant, he is a murderer and hence an Evildoer in the judgment of most persons. But in some societies, although infanticide as such may be judged evil, a few infants nevertheless are put to death *perhaps* only when they have not yet been perceived as human beings either because they have not been given names or because they have been born under conditions suggesting they are not human and must be destroyed.[1] The *perhaps* must be emphasized; members of the society may have given the anthropologist or whoever provides such an interpretation not the truth but the prevailing rationalization.[2]

Judgments concerning evil are not mysterious or unique inasmuch as they involve the same processes we postulate whenever one person attempts to understand and evaluate another person. The sequence begins with the stimulus or stimuli that are perceived in the outside world, includes an immediate or primary judgment, and may then lead to reflection and also a secondary but not necessarily final judgment. In addition, the Judge stores within himself certain values or predispositions that influence that perception and those subsequent judgments.[3] Human beings are seldom passive recipients of stimuli:

they hear a noise and try to interpret it; they see a mountain in the distance and call it beautiful or ominous. They try, in brief, to find meaning, however flimsy, in the environment and to appreciate what they perforce or deliberately perceive.

Stimuli can be examined by concentrating upon their content, magnitude, and temporal attributes. In terms of content, it is self-evident that any stimulus, human or not, may be related to the judgment of evil, however validly or invalidly. Here in fact is another reason why evil can be and is ubiquitous. Of course an individual may also judge himself. In any case, a potential or actual Evildoer or an evil-producing situation, as well as a potential or actual Victim, must be perceived or conceived before the judgment of evil is passed: one or more persons in the past, present, or future are perceived to be involved in robbery, cheating, attacking, discriminating, torturing—any verb associated with the psychological criterion of evil will do. Both the Evildoer and the Victim or either one may be present or absent, and their momentary relation to the Judge may affect his judgment. Is it more horrible to observe someone being tortured, to see the evildoing on television, or to hear or read about it? The question is most relevant, but the answer is not forthcoming: a fair summary of research and common sense suggests that it all depends. Being an eyewitness may make the details lively and compelling; but being a reader, viewer, or listener may enable the imagination to cast up even more ghastly fantasies.

The fact that evil can be visualized or anticipated in advance offers a vital clue to preventing and combating many of its manifestations. The most sweeping evil of our era or any era, for example, is war. On the basis of the experience of mankind, the banal assertion bears repeating: any war leads ultimately to conditions highly likely to result in evil for some persons, the victors as well as the vanquished, even though its exact nature may not be specified. The expectations concerning the conditions under which evil behavior occurs vary considerably. When the inhabitants of Tristan da Cunha, a small, isolated island in the south Atlantic, were evacuated to England after a volcano threatened their homes and land, they were compelled to learn not to trust strangers. A thief walked off with a sack of potatoes that one of them, assuming naively it would be safe, had left outside a store on a busy street. Crime for these people was simply "unbelievable."[4] A Judge must assume that the driver of the car heading toward him from the opposite direction will remain on the right side of the road (or on the left, if he lives in Britain or a British-influenced land) and not ram into him. But should he walk alone down a dark street of a modern city?

Magnitude, the second dimension, refers to the number of Evildoers or Victims and to the potentiality of situations to produce Victims en masse. Measures are available to assess natural situations, such as the force of the wind, the height of the river, the depth of the snow, the power of the earthquake. But a gentle breeze can initiate a violent forest fire, and a fierce wind can turn a mill that generates the power driving an emergency power plant of a hospital. Measuring devices also exist for social situations: price indexes, percentages of unemployed, scarcities of necessities. Evildoers, when they can be located, can also be counted. Was the murder committed by a single person or a gang? How many persons were responsible for the declaration of a war? Who are "the merchants of death" who profit from the conflict? Similarly the number of Victims varies. An epidemic strikes hundreds of persons, a murderer usually a single Victim and his immediate family or friends, although many additional unforeseen or unforeseeable consequences may arise. The seriousness of an accident *may* affect the responsibility a Judge assigns to the Victim.[5]

More than numbers influence the depth of perception. The Judge may perceive, or he may think he perceives, information concerning the background or motivation of the Evildoer or the Victim. He may try to ascertain the aspirations of the Victim's personality that have been allegedly damaged. Attention may be concentrated upon one particular person because of a belief that evil is contagious.

The third or temporal dimension includes both the duration and orientation of what is judged to be evil. The Judge perceives that the person he considers a Victim is experiencing a sharp, momentary pain or a dull but enduring pain. His own judgment concerning the elapsed time *may* depend not only upon clocks and calendars but also, when he introspects phenomenologically, upon his own age, the content of the interval being judged and his reactions to that content, his reason for making the judgment, the point in time at which the judgment is passed, and the standard he employs.[6]

Sometimes judgment is passed not only on persons but also on groups or nations—Sodom, Gomorrah, Admah, Zeboiim, Nazi Germany, Rhodesia. The Judge does not of course perceive, symbolically or actually, every member of such a community. He singles out a limited number of persons as the Evildoers and then generalizes his reaction to what he has perceived.

Since survival and satisfaction more often than not require participation in groups, the stimuli being judged frequently are derived from some kind of social interaction. Unquestionably every person who has not been segregated from society in a prison or a mental institution participates actively in a web of reciprocal and nonreciprocal obligations: families, other relatives, friends, social and political organizations, work groups, metaphysical associations. An attempt may be made to try to determine whether the outcome of such interactions is good or bad, whether the persons are Evildoers or Victims. Failure to keep one's promises, to discharge one's responsibilities, or to be honorable and honest usually induces an unfavorable reaction and a judgment.

Not only are groups judged, but they are also the stimuli likely to arouse appropriate values. In the company of clergymen, a Judge probably notes moral misdemeanors more frequently than when he is drinking with friends at a bar. Over a two-month period Canadian students *may* change some of their values when a computer has informed them concerning the modal values of the groups to which they belong.[7] Delinquent gangs in the United States *may* have subcultures of their own whose norms "run counter to the norms of the larger society."[8] Deeds the delinquents know to be evil in that larger society they *may* judge to be good among themselves, and some but not all the standards of the outer world they *may* call not evil but undesirable.[9] Such an easy, dramatic interpretation cannot be made with complete assurance, for *perhaps* some members of a delinquent subculture may experience guilt, some may reform, and most may not be immune to influences from the main culture.[10] Similarly in a complex society most individuals are affected by so-called reference groups to which they do not belong but to whose values or ways of behaving they subscribe.

The influence of values aroused by the group in which the Judge is participating or to which he refers his behavior suggests that not only does the external world of stimuli affect his judgments but also that his own predispositions play a major role in determining what he chooses to call evil. The Evildoer, as has been suggested, does not always wear horns;[11] he must be identified largely on the basis of the values the Judge has within himself. The predispositions explain in large part why individuals judge or evaluate stimuli so differently. Someone who is egocentric or rigid, for example, may be easily shocked and be inclined readily to perceive evil in innumerable persons or situations. Any belief may affect perception. If the Judge is Japanese and believes that human nature "is naturally good and to be trusted" and hence "does not need to fight an evil half of itself," he *may* be less likely to perceive evil in his milieu.[12] Since he would value highly the virtue of "fulfilling one's obligations," however, he must also be inclined to perceive evil in nonfulfillment rather than in human nature.

A fascinating problem is to try to determine the relative importance of the stimulus and a Judge's predispositions. The issue can be indicated in a quick sentence. At the instant a stone falls on your head, you are affected virtually completely by the stimulus; when you lose and then look for a small object like a contact lens or a key, what you perceive (notice, pay attention to) depends almost totally on your desire to find that object. The mixture varies.

The predispositions relevant to judging evil may vary from a simple prejudice to a set of values. Theologians and optimists, for example, may believe that goodness pervades the universe because the deity has so willed it; consequently, they are likely to perceive instances of goodness more frequently than those of evil. Or consider the varying conceptions of sin and hence evil summarized, perhaps too glibly, in an authoritative encyclopedia:

American Indian: "vice, crime, pollution, and even misfortune"
Babylonian: "an unconscious violation of the ceremonial regulations"
Buddhist: " 'folly,' as a result of ignorance"
Celtic: "gods being offended by neglect"
Chinese (Confucius): "theft, robbery, . . . malignity, perverseness, mendacity, vindictiveness, . . . vascillating weakness . . . , being unfilial"
Christian: "The explicit or implicit claim to live independently of God, to put something else, be it the world or self, in His place"
Egyptian: "murder, robbery, theft, oppression, impiety towards the gods and the dead, lying, slander, dishonesty, avarice, hasty temper, pride, loquacity, eavesdropping, adultery . . . masturbation, . . . injustice, partiality, disrespect for the aged and for parents, disobedience, contentiousness, rancour, ingratitude, selfishness, drunkenness"
Greek: "all conduct which by omission or by commission, in overt act or inner meaning, is offensive to the supra-human Powers"

Hebrew: "the performance or neglect of certain external acts"

Iranian: "a refusal, on the part of the free choice of the human will, to conform to the divine will"

Japanese (oldest Shinto): "breaking down the divisions of the rice-fields, filling up the irrigating channels, opening the flood-gates of sluices, sowing seed over again, planting wands, flaying alive and flaying backwards, evacuating excrements, . . . cutting the living skin, cutting the dead skin, white men, . . . a son's cohabitation with his own mother, a father's cohabitation with his own daughter, a man's cohabitation with his mother-in-law, a man's cohabitation with animals, calamity through crawling worms, calamity through the gods on high, calamity through birds on high, killing the animals, . . . performing witchcraft"

Muslim: "pride and opposition to God . . . infidelity or the ascribing of partners to God, murder, theft, adultery, unnatural crimes, neglect of the Ramadan fast and of the Friday prayers, magic, gambling, drunkenness, perjury, usury, disobedience to parents"

Roman: "enmity with superhuman forces"

Teutonic: "blasphemy, perjury, adultery"[13]

In addition, as is being repeatedly emphasized throughout this book, values fluctuate from society to society. In the West, stress is likely to be placed upon freedom of choice, but cultures exist in which "the concept is meaningless."[14] Within our own society, moreover, significant individual differences arise. Some persons believe that their destiny is controlled by external forces, others that they control their own destiny.[15] This so-called locus of control *may* mean that American college students differ with respect to whether they believe the world is "difficult," "unjust," "governed by luck," or "politically unresponsive."[16] Or when is political violence judged not to be evil in Western society? Some Judges *may* be predisposed to consider that violence may be justified as a method to protect or restore a system considered legitimate or to disrupt one deemed illegitimate; to impose what is considered to be a superior order on an out-group; to enable some other group such as a nation to have its own system and thus to achieve self-determination; to contribute to a desirable social order or to the enhancement of desirable personality traits.[17] From one or more of these alternatives all kinds of consequences may flow, especially in connection with the Judge's attitude toward war or his conviction concerning the relation between ends and means.

Whenever persons or situations are perceived—for example, in a discussion of contemporary issues—the Judge's values *may* not be invoked one by one but are likely to cohere.[18] The values predisposing him to be inclined to evaluate persons or situations in specific ways, moreover, may well be consistent, even though an outsider may think otherwise.

NOTES

1. Karl Duncker, "Ethical Relativity?" *Mind,* 48 (1939): 39-57.

2. Mary Douglas, *Purity and Danger* (New York: Praeger, 1966), p. 39.

3. Leonard W. Doob, *Pathways to People* (New Haven: Yale University Press, 1975).

4. Peter A. Munch, *Crisis in Utopia* (New York: Crowell, 1971), p. 220.

5. Ellen Berscheid and Elaine Hatfield Walster, *Interpersonal Attraction* (Reading, Mass.: Addison-Wesley, 1969), pp. 12-14.

6. Leonard W. Doob, *Patterning of Time* (New Haven: Yale University Press, 1971).

7. Milton Rokeach, "Long-Term Value Change Initiated by Computer Feedback," *Journal of Personality and Social Psychology,* 32 (1975): 467-76.

8. Richard A. Cloward and Lloyd E. Ohlin, *Delinquency and Opportunity* (Glencoe: Free Press, 1960), p. 1.

9. Nevill Sanford et al., eds., *Sanctions for Evil* (San Francisco: Jossey-Bass, 1971), p. ix. See also Travis Hirschi, *Causes of Delinquency* (Berkeley: University of California Press, 1972).

10. Gresham Sykes and David Matza, "Techniques of Neutralization," *American Sociological Review* 22 (1958): 664-70.

11. Erich Fromm, *The Anatomy of Human Destructiveness* (New York: Holt, Rinehart and Winston, 1973), p. 432.

12. Ruth Benedict, *The Chrysanthemum and The Sword* (Boston: Houghton Mifflin, 1946), p. 191.

13. James Hastings, ed., *Encyclopaedia of Religion and Ethics* (New York: Scribner's, 1922), pp. 528-71.

14. Dorothy Lee, *Freedom and Culture* (Englewood Cliffs: Prentice-Hall, 1959), p. 102.

15. Julian B. Rotter, "Generalized Expectancies for Internal versus External Control of Reinforcement," *Psychological Monographs* 80, no. 1 (1960): 609.

16. Barry E. Collins, "Four Components of the Rotter Internal-External Scale," *Journal of Personality and Social Psychology* 29 (1974): 381-91.

17. Kenneth W. Grundy and Michael A. Weinstein, *The Ideologies of Violence* (Columbus: Charles E. Merrill, 1974), pp. 14-15.

18. Laurence H. Tribe, Corine S. Schelling, and John Voss, *When Values Conflict* (Cambridge: Ballinger Publishing Company, 1976).

5

PRIMARY JUDGMENTS

Almost always the perceived person, group, or situation is immediately evaluated or judged. The judgment may be of various kinds, depending on what is perceived, the attitudes evoked by the stimuli, or the predispositions inducing or facilitating perception in the first place. The Judge is a living, responding individual, and therefore he seldom is indifferent to his first impressions. In a quest for meaning, he makes snap or at least not reflective judgments concerning other persons and situations—or himself.

To be sure, the one judgment of interest here involves that of right or wrong, good or bad, nonevil or evil. Each person, probably no matter where he lives, has a rich vocabulary to express such a judgment. Language in this respect is almost infinitely varied. There are proverbs, polite and obscene slang, legal terms, traditional phrases at the disposal of anyone who would praise or condemn what he has perceived.[1] Such labeling is obviously one of the supreme achievements of human beings, for language enables us efficiently to store information and misinformation. Since the idea of good and evil exists everywhere, that idea has a label, which is likely to be used whenever the appropriate occasion arises. An infinite regress is evident: the ubiquity of the phenomena of good and evil encourages the ubiquitous use of the terms *good* and *evil*, the ubiquitous labeling focuses attention upon, directs perception toward the phenomena. And our language tends to polarize our judgments, making it easier to pronounce "black" or "white" rather than, as it were, some hue in between.[2] Not in jest do I add the thought that phenomenologically we could abolish evil by prohibiting mankind from using the word in passing judgment; but even if the proposal were successful, another word would be found to refer to misery and taboo breaking.

Again attention must be called to the judgments that vary from society to society and from individual to individual within each society. The reasons for societal variability need not again detain us, since we have already indicated the complex nature of the explanations that are evoked. Even in a population as relatively homogeneous as American college students, moral judgments *may* be made on the basis of quite different ethical principles: some may consider their own personal conscience, others their social responsibility. These principles, moreover, may be related to personality traits in a loose sort of way; thus those students appealing to conscience *may* be more progressive, rebellious, unconventional, and socially active, whereas those concerned with social responsibility may be more good-natured, thoughtful, well socialized, somewhat conventional, and possessing a strong need for social order.[3] At the very least we have here another illustration of the fact that human beings never behave in a vacuum; they are somewhat organized, they have personalities.

This primary judgment, hasty though it be, may stem from the deeper predispositions within the Judge. Nonconformists, for example, are often considered Evildoers even when the taboos they allegedly violate are not believed by other Judges to be vital to the functioning of the society. One purist condemns nudists, another the use of slang. Even at this point in the judgmental process, however, the Judge may make a distinction between what social scientists used to call the folkways and the mores; violating the latter but not the former is judged to be sinful. If a person in our society uses his knife to carry food to his mouth, followers of prissy rules of etiquette consider him uncouth and greedy, though not evil. If he plunges a knife into his mother, he is an Evildoer—probably under almost all conceivable circumstances. Neither act meets with approval, but the first is simply discouraged: the second is taboo. The first is a minor infraction; the second is evil. Driving a car above the legal speed limit is an illegal act though unlikely to be called evil; the principle behind the regulation, to prevent ghastly accidents resulting from the driver's failure to show concern for human life, however, certainly must be considered a device to avoid evil.

In slightly different words, the Judge's predispositions produce within him an attitude toward the stimulus. When samples of children

were once asked what kinds of behavior they considered a "good" or
"bad" thing to do, those from five American Indian tribes seemed to
favor "regard for others" and "service" since "goodness and badness
for the child lie primarily in how he relates himself to other people."
Another Indian sample inclined toward "competence" and "personal
virtues," since their society tended to emphasize "work and industrious-
ness." And a sample of American children in the Midwest approved
"self-restraint" and "regard for others," since their goal seemed to be
"to adjust one's own impulses to the group demands, to maximize
gratification while minimizing conflict with others."[4] "Bad" behavior,
however, is not necessarily evil. Although parents may make a
distinction between the two when they judge their children's behavior,
they perhaps also feel that in the long run "naughty" behavior has
"evil" consequences either for the society or the children's character.

The Judge's attitude or predispositions affecting his judgment may be
dormant until he is confronted with the stimulus. An epithet is supplied
within a communication or its source is given, as a result of which a
favorable or unfavorable attitude is immediately evoked. The Evildoer
expresses remorse, in which case the Judge's primary or secondary
judgment *may* be less harsh. Common sense may not be a reliable guide
to predicting the effect of information. Knowing that an Evildoer comes
from an impoverished or a comfortable background *may* not affect the
judgment of American college students.[5]

The reference group to which the Judge belongs, provided it is
salient, is likely to affect the person or persons in the situation with
whom he identifies or feels sympathy and hence his primary judgment.
From his window or on a television screen, he sees a police squad preventing a group of young people from marching down a street. If the
Judge is a policeman, he will immediately consider the police innocent
and the marchers Evildoers. But if he knows the marchers and subscribes to their viewpoint, they will be judged the Victim and the police
Evildoers. As I watched the gunfire between the Cypriot police and the
men staging the coup against the Cyprus government in 1974—the
incident that forced me to consider the problem of evil—I think I
identified with neither group, but the dead bodies produced a judgment
of evil concerning—well, I am not so sure.

The primary judgment can involve a Victim only indirectly, for
frequently it is the means the Evildoer employs that are judged. Those

means include deprivation in a physical sense: torture, death, starvation, any kind of deprivation. On a psychological level almost any device may be utilized; the range is from blustering threats to the kindest words that elicit anxiety or guilt.[6] In the mass media, according to the judgments of some persons in society, many forms of advertising, most pornography, and the communication of falsehoods and scandal are judged to induce or facilitate evil behavior and thus eventually to produce Victims. Even before the Victims are located, they are considered evil.

The Judge may make an effort not to perceive the individual as a Victim when others do so. If that Victim is given some kind of reward as compensation, he *may* become a non-Victim in the eyes of the beholder.[7] Also, a secondary judgment may render him a non-Victim when it is felt that he deserves to suffer or that he himself is responsible for his suffering. Evil thus evaporates by means of judgment.

A basic puzzle to solve is the discovery of the principle employed by the Judge to pass a primary judgment. One or both persons in a simple transaction, for example, *may* feel that inequity is involved,[8] particularly when "an obverse relation" is perceived between what each believes he contributes and receives, or they *may* feel that "a norm of reciprocity," said also to be "universal," has been violated.[9] *Perhaps* the Judge shows greater concern for his own equity than he does for that of the person he is appraising.[10] Societies, too, have principles that pervade their members, on the basis of which primary judgments concerning the presence or absence of evil is perceived. An extreme, dramatic, perhaps melodramatic illustration is that of the Ik in Uganda who no longer are permitted by the authorities to be hunters, as a result of which they apparently survive by following a principle which we in the West would call almost completely selfish. For example:

[A pleasant youth, suffering from starvation] was found the day after he should have returned [from a trip] high up on the last peak of the trail before it descends to Pirre, cold and dead. Then you could see how thin he was, or so I was told, for those who found him took the things he had been carrying, pushed his body into the bus and left it. "Why bother carrying him back? He was dead!" they said as they distributed the goods. [His] wife came out to see what she could get for herself, her son was playing with other children, and paid no attention, only his mother just sat and stared, and who knows what she was thinking about?

... men would watch a child with eager anticipation as it crawled toward the fire, then burst into gay and happy laughter as it plunged a skinny hand into the coals. Such times were the few times when parental affection showed itself; a mother would glow with pleasure to hear such joy occasioned by her offspring, and pull it tenderly out of the fire.

When Bila was suffering most from her infected breast, which dripped pus over her nursing child or the food she was eating, she cared neither about herself nor anyone else. She acknowledged that it was unclean and unhealthy, and when told that she could spread illness to others in this way, her own family, she looked amazed—amazed not that illness could be spread like this but amazed that anyone should think she should worry about spreading it. When, at its height, Bila was in great pain and was sitting outside the [gateway] crying, holding her breast under which a little puddle of pus and blood had formed, Atum, her father, took notice of her only to ask her if she had to sit there—she was blocking the entrance and her crying gave him a headache.[11]

Certainly the judgments of the Ik concerning a dead, an immature, and a suffering person may be extreme, but they indicate the extent to which judgments are affected by societal norms resulting from extreme conditions.

One principle that immediately gives rise to a primary judgment of evil is self-evident. Can any principle, a devil's advocate must ask, be self-evident? Perhaps the skeptical reader has already discovered the principle within himself as he read about the Ik. If not, I think he will come upon it more certainly whenever he experiences the torturing of another human being either directly or vicariously. Instances are too easy to find; I select one from the regime of the colonels in Greece (1967-74) not because Greece at that time was more atrocity prone than any other country with an authoritarian regime and a secret police but because this horror is reported as "documentary material" by a sincere, reliable person who was also tortured by the same regime and because I happened upon her book as I was thinking about Cyprus and this principle. It was "handwritten and smuggled out of" prison by a thirty-year-old man, a graduate of a Greek university. Without, I hope, wishing to be sadistic—or masochistic, for that matter—I quote it in its entirety so that the reader's own horror will not be truncated:

I was arrested by members of the General Security Police of Athens on January 3rd, 1971 ...

They entered my apartment at about 8 p.m., pointing a revolver at me. As soon as they arrested me they started to hit me and to make threats such as, "We are going to kill you," and, "We are going to throw you from the top of Mount Parnis."

At the headquarters of the security police, they tortured me, first in an office. They punched me on the face and in the stomach, gave me electric shocks and poked my eyes with their fingers. My nose started bleeding as a result of the blows.

They then took me up to the terrace. I was tied on to a bench, half naked, and they started to hit the soles of my feet with an iron bar. Some of the policemen sat on my chest while one of them, whom I recognized as Gravaritis, hit my genitals and other parts of my body with a stick. He also punched me on the head with both hands or sometimes stuffed a wet cloth on a stick into my mouth in order to smother my cries. Another policeman was squeezing my testicles with his hand. The pain made me writhe, and the ropes cut into my ankles. I was then untied and two policemen held me and forced me to walk around while they swore at me. They then released me and started to throw me one to the other, and then two policemen would pull at my arms in opposite directions. They tied me on to the bench and the whole process of falanga and beating started again, and was repeated about four times.

Then I was taken into an office, and they started to hit me again. They made me stand with one arm in the air, like the Statue of Liberty, and I kept falling down. A policeman was hitting my genitals. They put me on a chair and started to hit me again.

They then threw me into a cell and left me lying on the cement floor. During the next days Gravaritis would take me out into an office and hit me. His favourite tortures were to poke my eyes with his fingers, grab me by the hair and bang my head against the wall, and punch me on the head and inflict tortures on my genitals with his hands.

While this was going on, I could hear the screams of people being tortured, which grew louder all the time. I could hear names being called for questioning. In my cell I heard continuously my name being called for interrogation. I heard the cries of the others who had been accused with me being tortured; I heard them being murdered by being thrown through a trapdoor into the basement. I was delirious all the time.

Because I was in this state a doctor was sent to look at me. I was even shown one of those accused with me to prove that they had not been killed.

There were about seven policemen present at my tortures, of whom I can give the names of only three: Gravaritis, Kalivas and Smailis.[12]

I phrase the principle as follows: torturing of this sort is evil because I would not want it to happen to me, to anyone I love, in fact to anyone.

Or perhaps: I am afraid that it could happen. I do not want it to happen, nor do you, on the basis of both criteria of evil: the pain and the violation of human integrity. And yet the horror evoked by such ghastly gore, I must add, is also fascinating, or at least it fascinates some persons. Why? We shall tangle with this problem later on.

In the meantime let it be noted again that no person is judged an Evildoer or a situation evil producing unless a causal sequence resulting in one or more Victims can be uncovered. Man has no direct control, usually, over natural events (hurricanes, cyclones, droughts, floods, unusual fluctuations in weather), which may have effects more disastrous than those wrought by human Evildoers: people drown or are otherwise killed; homes and shops are destroyed or looted; psychic trauma is experienced for years afterward. A hurricane at sea having absolutely no discerning effect upon human beings is like the noise from the philosopher's tree falling in a deserted forest and hence, since it has no psychological existence, it is not ordained to be judged evil.

Man-made situations that potentially or actually give rise to Victims, however, may be judged evil even when no discernible Victim is in sight; for, other things being equal, they are so perfectly correlated with human misery that inevitably they deserve to be judged evil. The situations are not easy to specify, but as a hypothesis I propose that they include sharp inequality, poverty, and alienation. Sharp inequality heads the list because the unequal distribution of goods, services, and honors in a society, according to the view at least of egalitarians, makes those receiving minor shares unhappy and violates a basic human right—living in comfort and dignity. Although inequality, whether general, traditional, or artificial, is an unavoidable fact of existence in every society, a sharp division between the haves and have-nots most certainly produces frustration and eventually unrest. The consequences thus are evil according to a social-moral criterion.

Poverty, another external circumstance, means that there are poverty-stricken persons experiencing misery. They are judged to be Victims unless the Judge believes that the poor, whether free or slaves, are essential for the well-being of the society. Another Judge, however, may maintain that their suffering places them in the category of Victims or that their misery is likely to facilitate evildoing. Such primary judgments, however, can produce contradictory or dissonant reactions. Liberal Judges in the West, for example, approve of the way newly independent nations seek to develop their own resources in order to alleviate poverty, but they also note that corruption and bribery persist, even increase, and that poverty for the masses is not reduced.[13] And—the devil's advocate speaks again—poverty may goad some persons to be educated or to migrate, consequences not likely to be judged evil but not necessarily justifying the condition itself.

The third category, alienation, is ambiguous. It may refer to the powerlessness experienced by individuals when they contemplate their own destiny, to a lack of clarity concerning what should be believed, to the conviction that socially disapproved actions are required to achieve particular goals, to a feeling of isolation resulting from the assigning of a low value to activities highly valued in the society, or to self-estrangement, which in turn has various meanings ranging from the feeling that one's own self is alien to the loss of meaningful satisfactions.[14] In any of these five forms alienation produces some kind of misery or conflict, and hence in our society the ensuing conduct is probably judged to be evil both on psychological and social-moral grounds.

Again and again the Judge is content with his primary judgment. He knows what evil is, and so his judgment is easily forthcoming when he perceives, directly or indirectly, one or more Evildoers and Victims. The case for him is closed. But on occasion he reflects or is compelled to reflect and to make a secondary judgment.

NOTES

1. May Edel and Abraham Edel, *Anthropology and Ethics* (Cleveland: Case Western Reserve University Press, 1968), p. 121.

2. Alfred Korzybski, *Science and Sanity* (Lancaster: International Non-Aristotelian Library Publishing Company, 1933).

3. Robert Hogan, "A Dimension of Moral Judgment," *Journal of Consulting and Clinical Psychology* 35 (1970):205-12.

4. Robert J. Havighurst and Bernice L. Neugarten, *American Indian and White Children* (Chicago: University of Chicago Press, 1955), pp. 111-13.

5. Michael G. Rumsey, "Effects of Defendant Background and Remorse on Sentencing Judgments," *Journal of Applied Social Psychology* 6 (1976): 64-68.

6. Philip P. Hallie, *The Paradox of Cruelty* (Middletown: Wesleyan University Press, 1969), pp. 24-26.

7. Melvin J. Lerner, "The Desire for Justice and Reactions to Victims," in J. Macaulay and L. Berkowitz, eds., *Altruism and Helping Behavior* (New York: Academic Press, 1970), pp. 205-29.

8. J. Stacy Adams, "Toward an Understanding of Inequity," *Journal of Abnormal and Social Psychology* 67 (1963): 422-36.

9. Alvin W. Gouldner, "The Norm of Reciprocity," *American Sociological Review* 25 (1960): 161-78.

10. Irving Lane and Lawrence A. Messé, "Distribution of Insufficient, Sufficient, and Oversufficient Rewards," *Journal of Personality and Social Psychology* 2 (1972): 228-33.

11. Colin M. Turnbull, *The Mountain People* (New York: Simon & Schuster, 1972), pp. 89, 112, 218.

12. Amalia Fleming, *A Piece of Truth* (Boston: Houghton Mifflin, 1973), pp. 248-49.

13. Ronald Wraith and Edgar Simpkins, *Corruption in Developing Countries* (New York: Norton, 1963).

14. Melvin Seeman, "On the Meaning of Alienation," *American Sociological Review* 24 (1959): 783-91.

6

SECONDARY JUDGMENTS

Primary or snap judgments concerning evil may be revised as the Judge considers the reasons for those judgments. He may feel instantly that a particular person is an Evildoer or a Victim, but then he may wonder why he has passed this judgment. He may even seek to explain that individual's behavior. The challenge of this chapter is to delineate the factors affecting reflection and the ensuing secondary judgments.

External factors that can induce revised judgments are not at the focus of attention during this analysis. But they may play a role, for the human being or the situation being judged often changes over time, and the Judge perceives the change. The apparent Evildoer may turn out to be on the side of the angels. Whether such shifts, whether social changes in general can be related to identifiable factors is a conundrum beyond our present scope. One cannot be certain. Still it seems at least provocative to assume a deterministic approach to this problem of variability: some cause-and-effect sequence is likely to be discovered. The search, however, can be tenuous. A historian, for example, attempts to show how "two modern revolutions, bourgeois and proletariat," have found acceptance in Japan because they "have appeared to the Japanese so comprehensive and so capable of application to the Japanese experience."[1] But, methodologically, this is like praising a child who says that a pair of mittens fits because his hands are the right size after he has stated that his hands are comfortable inside of them.

One clear-cut reason for revising primary judgments stems from the facile way in which language can be employed. It is tempting to forget the fact that most behavior is likely to fall along a continuum and instead to think in terms of dichotomies, such as justice-injustice, equality-inequality, virtue-vice, good-evil. The presence of these dichotomies leads to the conviction that modes of behavior can be thoroughly or instantly praised or condemned or that they should be followed or avoided. Reflection suggests that from time to time some of the deeds committed in the name of good values held by religious missions in developing countries, by judges meting out punishment to convicted criminals, or by politicians in the name of patriotism or economy are not completely good and unquestionably contain elements of evil.

This act of labeling may be almost instantaneous, or it may occur after reflection. Probably epithets appear as primary judgments: an alleged Evildoer is immediately labeled a criminal, a communist, a reactionary, and so forth. Secondary judgments, on the other hand, require assessment and hence a delay. A judge who is opposed to violence and considers it evil *may* first have to decide whether the actions of a group merit that designation, and his decision may depend upon the goal of the group and his own feelings about that goal.[2]

Fine distinctions between good and evil may be discouraged by the Judge's own predispositions, which in turn reflect the view prevailing in his society. According to a very broad generalization, for example, in India and China, "there is no mighty historical struggle between the spirits of good and evil, light and darkness." Instead man's problem is "to realize his true identity with the divine, to search for and bring out his inner divinity by peeling off the veils of illusion": the extinction of the ego is "an essential step on the way to the discovery of one's fundamental identity with the individualized divinity within the self."[3] One wonders whether a starving Indian or a Chinese in pain actually subscribes to such a judgment during moments of agony or despair.

Dialectical reasoning leads to a similar disposition: a process like evil cannot exist without its opposite, which is good, and a synthesis is likely to occur.[4] It is relatively easy, however, to discover other formulations asserting that good and evil are closely related or even hopelessly intertwined. An Arab says at the outset of a discourse on the subject, "Of the good in you I can speak, but not of the evil/For what is evil but good tortured by its own hunger and thirst?" There follows one metaphor after another indicating that the line between the two is thin and wavering:

You are good when you are one with yourself.
Yet when you are not one with yourself you are not evil.

For a divided house is not a den of thieves; it is only
a divided house.
And a ship without rudder may wander aimlessly among
perilous isles yet sink not to the bottom. . . .

. . . You are good when you are fully awake in your speech.
Yet you are not evil when you sleep while your tongue staggers
without purpose.
And even stumbling speech may strengthen a weak tongue. . . .

You are good in countless ways, and you are not evil when
you are not good.
You are only loitering and sluggard.
Pity that the stags cannot teach swiftness to the turtles.[5]

The prophet who is speaking suggests that there are standards for good-ness, from which evil departs not in an absolute but in an almost quanti-tative sense.

The mixture of what is judged to be good or evil can indeed be em-bodied in a single person. The Evildoer may be like Satan who pretends to be good in order to be popular, to be worshipped as another angel.[6] Or the individual is judged to be good and evil because he has attributes causing the Judge to make both judgments or because he is able to con-ceal or repress one of his attitudes. On a very theological level, the Judge may believe that God sometimes permits Satan or his equivalent to take possession of human beings since He "prefers to extract good from evil rather than to suppress evil entirely," and hence He grants special help after possession.[7] Similarly, a psychoanalyst contends that "whenever good is experienced, evil is also present," that "coming to terms with evil is . . . a moral task which calls for the highest exertions on the part of the ego," and that "whenever creative expression becomes an inner necessity, evil is also constellated."[8]

The mingling of good and evil creates a problem for a Judge who approves or disapproves of two apparently unrelated values and finds them on occasion to be interrelated. Suppose, for example, war is judged to be evil and scientific discoveries good. Statistically, it appears that wars in which England or Russia has engaged *may* have encouraged such discoveries in the next generation; for Spain, the opposite relation may have been true; for France, wars and the discoveries may have been concurrent in the same generation; for the Netherlands, the discoveries may have discouraged wars in the next generation; and for Germany and Italy, no significant relationships between the two phenomena may have existed.[9] What is a Judge to say about war if he wants new discoveries in science and if he would also have war abolished? His answer must depend on the country being examined, on whether he believes that reasoning from past associations is a valid guide to the future, on whether he has confidence in statistically established relations, and on whether he really considers scientific discoveries to be of equal value or all wars to be bad. In any case, the Judge would do well to pause and reflect.

Whether good and evil are viewed as discrete or along a continuum, the Judge also reflects upon his own conception of evil per se. Fate, for example, may be regarded as evil, as it seems to have been among the ancient Greeks, but not among Hindus and Japanese.[10] Sometimes disagreements among Judges may be a matter of definition and semantics. In our society everyone agrees that murder is wrong under most circumstances. The thorny question of abortion then hinges largely on the definition of human life. At what point can the fetus be considered a human being? The moment it is labeled human, according to one viewpoint, performing an abortion is evil. But another value, say proponents of abortion, may be the life of the mother, the willingness of the parents to have the child (which can affect the way they treat him or her during infancy and thereafter), the marital status of the mother, and so forth.

Reflection may also occur after facts have been collected and collated. Evidence is accumulated before the individual is judged guilty. A complicated illustration concerns the Society of the Great Way of Japan, which around 1885 proclaimed that the "spirit of our country is found in the three religions of Shinto, Confucianism, and Buddhism," which had enabled Japan to stimulate, respectively, "loyalty to the Emperors and love for our country," "to deal with the affairs of the world," and to cope with "world passions." But Evildoers within Japan must have been detected, for it was also indicated that "in recent times the work of former Emperors has been destroyed, the spirit of the state is being undermined, the organization of society is being disturbed and the basis of morals is being weakened."[11]

Probably every Judge at some time or other confronts the ancient (if hackneyed) question of means and ends: can ever the latter justify the former and hence exonerate the person being judged from becoming an Evildoer? The same problem exists whenever there is a conflict in values or alternate actions. Abraham, a philosopher has reminded us, believed that God commanded him to suspend the taboo against murdering one's own son, and hence he allowed a command, coming from God, to take precedence over his own knowledge that he would be judged evil under almost all circumstances in every society and by himself. For simple persons like us, our philosophical guide adds, the question that must be answered when we would suspend or violate a morally good impulse is, "Are you really addressed by the Absolute or by one of his apes?"[12] In less cosmic form the same kind of "teleological suspension of the ethical"—a fine phrase that calls attention to a faith that a "particular" act is "higher than the universal" principle seemingly applicable to it—is invoked whenever persons seek to justify an act that is ordinarily disapproved.[13] Even Marx, opposed as he was to war, made an exception for conflicts "fought in service of 'progress.'"[14]

Although evil exists only in the eyes of the beholder, a disapproved activity or situation is not necessarily judged to be evil. Reflection is necessary. The young child who spills his milk upon a precious rug may be judged naughty or inept, not evil; his act causes a minor pain (the psychological criterion) but does not seem to threaten an eternal value (the social-moral criterion). But suppose a person who has been offended steals into a house and deliberately empties a bottle of ink upon that rug? The judgment, therefore, depends not on a single factor like disapproval but on a host of other ones. The longer the duration of an event, for example, the more approval or disapproval that *may* be evoked.[15] One or more demographic factors *may* be involved, such as the Judge's sex.[16] Or the judgment *may* be affected by whether it is thought the accused intended to do what he did.[17] For reasons such as these, the Judge reflects upon the conditions surrounding the stimulus constellation he would judge. Somehow the social-moral criterion is rendered relevant.

The thorny question of responsibility and intention can no longer be avoided. Among Western Christians the view of Theologic Man prevails that evildoing is a deliberate act occurring after the Evildoer or the leader of the group has exercised free will by considering the alternatives. Children, imbeciles, the hopelessly insane, and those under the influence of drugs, external pressures, and overwhelming passions are therefore exempt. There is thus a relation between the views of religion regarding intention and the law regarding responsibility. Those not branded Evildoers or criminals may cause pain and suffering, and they may violate basic values—both criteria for evil—but what they do is excused; their actions are unintended evil. On a much more mundane level, any reason for believing that the individual "is not himself today" serves as a reason to excuse behavior that would otherwise be utterly condemned.

Aside from the exemptions just mentioned, it is not simple to affix responsibility or to absolve individuals of responsibility. That young child who damages property is judged to be only naughty, but his parents may be considered Evildoers for not foreseeing or preventing the misdemeanor. At what age is a person held responsible for his action? That question is like asking when a child becomes an adult. The reply differs from society to society or even, within the United States, from state to state. Whether the Judge is a Christian or not, he may be inclined to condemn "the evil of a free intelligent agent which chooses what is known to be morally wrong" and to find excuses for the individual who is not "free" or "intelligent."[18] Theologic Man is thus refined a trifle.

In Western society, therefore, a Judge may hold an individual culpable only when he thinks his action was deliberately intended. The critical factor *may* be the Judge's own age or stage of development; for example, adults may have a slight tendency to assign greater responsibility to environmental factors under some circumstances than do children.[19] The Judge's philosophy of causation (whether he thinks that he or outside forces control his destiny), however, *may* not affect his attribution of responsibility[20] but *may* influence the assistance he renders someone he judges to be a Victim.[21]

The conception of intention is neither simple nor straightforward. I turn to two Western philosophers and offer an abbreviated summary of what they have to say concerning a very simple act. A man wishes to attract the attention of the speaker during a meeting:

Because of this wish, he fidgets, and fidgeting may attract the attention he seeks. But does he fidget deliberately to achieve that end? He may or may not believe that fidgeting can serve as a communications medium. If he did not have the belief, then fidgeting must have been unintentional. If he has the belief but if he did not wish to use the medium, he might have fidgeted anyhow as a result of nervousness. Or with the belief he might have deliberately fidgeted and then ceased after discovering that he had not achieved his end.[22]

Fidgeting probably is seldom if ever considered an evil act, but the same kinds of problems arise in connection with more cosmic forms of behavior. Can one say, for example, that a motorist who exceeded the speed limit intended to kill a pedestrian who happened to be crossing the road? Like so much of communication and propaganda,[23] evil resulting from attaining a goal may be unintended and a by-product; a Victim "may be just as much ruined by a well-meaning father as he is by a sadist."[24]

In many social contexts the individual's responsibility cannot be judged with dispatch. This difficulty arises especially when the Judge perceives the fact that the individual being judged belongs to a community possessing a ready-made machine, such as discrimination against a minority or a form of persecution, requiring him to behave in a manner that makes him appear to be an Evildoer. Under these circumstances, the Judge may think that the individual may be unaware of the evil he is committing, that he may earnestly feel he is acting normally or obeying God's will. Prior to the American Civil War, the following advertisement appeared in a New Orleans newspaper:

NEGROES FOR SALE—a negro woman, 24 years of age, and her two children, one eight and the other three years old. Said negroes will be sold SEPARATELY or together, *as desired.* The woman is a good seamstress. She will be sold low for cash, or EXCHANGED FOR GROCERIES. For terms, apply to Matthew Bliss & Co., 1 Front Levee.[25]

Presumably Matthew Bliss or the owner of the woman and her two children were Christians. Is it sufficient to say that slavery at the time was institutionalized in the South, and therefore the sale of human beings was both legal and legitimatized? Probably not, if ever we are to find the roots of evil. But it is important to suggest that the seller must somehow have reconciled his treatment of Negroes with his Christian background and training.[26] Profit alone would not account for what any Judge today would call his evil behavior. The Negro for him was an essential ingredient of the economic system, a system that received almost universal approval in the South. He must have been perceived as not quite human or at least devoid of or deficient in human emotions. Since they were not human, blacks could be sold like cattle. If the "negro woman" being offered for sale were devoid of human emotion, she would not object to being bought separately, or she would recover from the loss of her children more quickly than would a mother with a white skin. The owner could thus rationalize the sale, and, since the rationalization was provided and reinforced by his society, he could well have believed either interpretation. Christian principles, after all, apply to human beings and not to animals or organisms that are not quite human. In some immediate or sociological sense, therefore, Mr. Bliss may not be judged responsible because he was following conventional practices. But can we really thus exonerate him?

The question just posed is more metaphysical than rhetorical, for we are really wishing to know, most crucially, the bases for a decision concerning whether a person accused of evil has considered "the alternatives" and thus, according to the Christian view, demonstrated free will as Theologic Man is supposed to do. One who deliberately avoids hearing an opinion contrary to his own may possibly seem culpable until an effort is made to account for his behavior. Perhaps no alternative was available; perhaps he had been taught in school or by his parents that the alternatives were to be avoided for compelling reasons. His mentors in this instance could be held ultimately responsible for making him an Evildoer. Or he might have considered various alternatives very carefully and then have come to the "wrong" conclusion according to some Judge now or in the future. Who is really to blame?

Individuals within a society and also societies themselves differ with respect to the responsibility they assign the person whose behavior is judged. Roughly two months after his conviction in 1971 for his role in the My Lai incident ("an unknown or uncounted number of Vietnamese civilians—old men, women, children, babies—perhaps more than five hundred" were killed by an American patrol),[27] a random sample of American civilians was asked whether they approved of bringing to trial the man in charge of that patrol, Lieutenant William Calley. About one-third said they believed he should have been tried because he had "no right to kill defenseless civilians" and because the trial "put across the important idea that every man must bear responsibility for his own action." Over half, however, disapproved because—again only the modal reasons are mentioned—it was "unfair to send a man to fight in Vietnam and then put him on trial for doing his duty" or "to single out one man" and thus use him as "a scapegoat."[28] Some of the important ethical issues of that war and of our times, consequently, were focused upon his trial—and people disagreed with one another.

Many individual differences result from the interaction between traits the Judges attribute to the Victim and their own expectations concerning the behavior associated with those traits. In our society *perhaps* a Victim who is considered respectable is more likely to be judged responsible for his condition than if he is less valued: the respectable Victim, the Judge may reason, does not in theory merit the misfortune because he must have a good character and hence he himself must be responsible and judged more harshly.[29] Other Judges may disagree and not link respectability and responsibility in this fashion, especially if they live in a non-Western culture; and as ever, the sex of the Judge *may* affect his judgment.[30]

Attributions of responsibility can be grouped along a continuum ranging from virtually no responsibility or fatalism to freewill or voluntarism at least under specified conditions. The position of the Judge along that continuum affects the judgment he makes concerning evildoing. At one extreme a devotee of astrology who is convinced that much or most behavior is determined by the position of the stars at one's birth may judge an Evildoer less harshly. At the other extreme it is possible (though not necessarily so) that devotees of deterministic doctrines may pass more lenient judgments. Among some of the thinkers in classical Greece, for example, there was a strong belief in determinism of various kinds (phrased in terms of causality, the gods, or fate in general), which served as the intellectual background against which freedom could be measured and contrasted and then responsibility and punishment be assigned.[31] Even Greece's Olympian deities, including Zeus himself, were virtually impotent. Time and time again they had to yield to "implacable fate." Later "woman [was considered] as the root of all evil and source of human misery."[32] The Nuer of West Africa fall between the two extreme postulates of fatalism and Theologic Man. They believe that anyone following the society's rules can avoid "not all misfortunes, for some misfortunes come to one and all alike, but those extra and special misfortunes which come from *dueri*, faults, and are to be regarded as castigations." And so they feel that "if misfortune comes to a man, it is most likely on account of some fault" of his. Yet if the offense is an unwitting one, they "do not . . . blame the man" (even though "they fear the consequences"); rather "they are sorry for him."[33]

The attitude of the Judge toward the category into which he fits the individual's behavior also influences his judgment. He may feel, for example, that overt aggression is closely correlated with evildoing. When, then, does he consider another person aggressive and hence, perhaps, an Evildoer? The person *may* be called aggressive, it seems, and consequently a candidate for negative evaluation or punishment only when he is unable to offer an acceptable excuse for his behavior; when he seems to have one or more alternatives open to him other than to be aggressive; when he does not condemn his own conduct; when he is reacting to a nonaggressive model; or when he is thought to be deliberately and unjustifiably harming a Victim.[34]

Another category affects the Judge's attribution of responsibility: the seriousness of the behavioral consequences of the actions associated with the other individual or individuals. *Perhaps* more responsibility is ordinarily assigned as seriousness increases,[35] but the reverse *may* be true when the Judge presumably assumes that a serious accident could not have been intended by its perpetrator—and the objective being or not being achieved by the alleged Evildoer may be taken into account.[36] Either of these two conflicting generalizations cannot easily be applied to cataclysmic events that, most Judges believe, result in dreadful evil. I would consider one event that led to the death of 135,000 persons and the destruction of large parts of a major city: the British and American air attacks on Dresden in the spring of 1945. A British air marshal has written the following about the raids:

That the bombing of Dresden was a great tragedy none can deny. That it was really a military necessity few . . . will believe. It was one of those terrible things that sometimes happen in wartime, brought about by an unfortunate combination of circumstances. Those who approved it were neither wicked nor cruel, though it may well be that they were too remote from the harsh realities of war to understand fully the appalling destructive power of air bombardment.[37]

Who, then, can be held responsible for the "biggest single massacre in European history"?[38] One can point to the Germans themselves since they had mercilessly bombed cities like Rotterdam and Coventry; but the Germans could say that bombing of civilians really began in one of their own cities, Freiburg (although it appears probable that this raid was not carried out by French but by German planes whose pilots had made a serious navigational error).[39] Responsibility must be assigned to the British and American authorities; but they wished to help their Soviet allies and thus to convince them that they would not turn against them. They also sought to terrorize Germany so that the war would end sooner with fewer losses. Who finally permitted the raid to occur? The British Air Ministry apparently checked with Winston Churchill, but it is unclear whether in fact he gave his consent.[40] If he did, he could be held immediately responsible for the situation itself—but again the background of the entire war and what he might have thought to be best for the British empire, Europe, and perhaps the world must have influenced him. The men who did the actual bombing could correctly say they were simply obeying orders, and they themselves had fleeting misgivings concerning the firebombing. After a squadron had been briefed in connection with the second wave of planes, "some of the aircrew who had been to Dresden before the war felt a little unhappy that such a raid was necessary."[41] When interviewed later, two of the men reported their feelings during the raid; the first was a bombardier, the second a Jewish pilot:

It was the only time I ever felt sorry for the Germans, but my sorrow lasted only for a few seconds; the job was to hit the enemy and to hit him very hard.

* * *

The fantastic glow from two hundred miles away grew ever brighter as we moved into the target. At 20,000 feet we could see details in the unearthly blaze that had never been visible before; for the first time in many operations I felt sorry for the population below.[42]

We can say, of course, that the people of Dresden were the Victims of the evil of war, but that phrase conceals the problem of assigning final responsibility, probably an insoluble problem unless some basic assumption is made. Were Hitler and the Nazis ultimately responsible? Perhaps, but who was responsible for them? Their parents, the Treaty of Versailles, the worldwide depression of the early thirties? On and on the story could go, or further and further backwards.

We cannot leave such atrocities unjudged. We dare not say, as some Judges in effect do, that a given bit of barbarism "never happened and besides they deserved it,"[43] for that is glib and meaningless. Nor is it helpful to point to other crimes besides those of Mr. Bliss (the slave merchant), Lieutenant Calley, Adolf Eichmann, the Germans who executed over three hundred Italians in the Ardeatine caves outside Rome in March 1944, and many others who consider themselves innocent of evil because their intentions are socially acceptable to their peers.[44] Call the evil they commit "banal," if you will, but surely it must also be contended that Evildoers cannot be separated completely from their deeds because they have succumbed to an order from a "higher" authority or from their own nasty unconscious. And yet—the argument with oneself spirals—should we not keep searching for the original, the ultimate Evildoers?

The Judge may raise the question of responsibility with reference to the actual or potential Evildoer but also to the Victim.[45] In order to maintain his belief in what he considers to be a just world, he may assign responsibility to the Victim for his own misery. The Victim, it is sometimes said, "is at fault, although through no fault of his own."[46] The Judge may observe that a human being is suffering or is being treated unjustly; he may locate the agent, the Evildoer, or the situation, and yet may withhold the judgment of evil. He may wish to believe in the existence of that just world: good must (and will) triumph. I myself am not the least amazed when other Judges sneer at such a notion after viewing centuries of the deeds of Satan, as it were, and particularly his accomplishments during the present century. What evidence is there for the victory of virtue?

A Judge considering a human being to be a Victim may or may not have sympathy with him. His conviction concerning the Victim's responsibility as well as his own may influence his judgment. Sometimes he or some other Judge obtains satisfaction from the existence of evil, and in a sense he is grateful to both the Evildoer and the Victim. Cotton Mather played an active role in the persecution of the so-called witches in Salem and elsewhere in Massachusetts in 1692; he attended the trials and wrote a book about them. "His righteous indignation that such things could be," it is said of him more than two centuries later, "was unconsciously submerged in the thrill of having been present as spectator at a collision between heaven and hell." Indeed, "the witchcraft was one experience that [he] would not willingly have foregone."[47] I remember seeing long lines of persons in London during the summer of

1945 waiting to enter theaters to see atrocity pictures of the Nazi concentration camps. Murder stories, the more gruesome the better, sell newspapers, or editors probably have that belief when they headline and otherwise feature such events. The Victims in these instances bring joy to bystanders who know they have played no role in inflicting the suffering. Those who are thus pleased, however, including Cotton Mather, may become Evildoers, for they are likely to be corrupted by their perversion—I must use the harsh word, if not completely accurately—and thus are inclined either to imitate or tolerate the evil they witness.

A very special case arises when the Judge passes judgment upon himself, as all good Theologic Men are supposed to do: does he consider himself an Evildoer or a Victim in some respect? Quite obviously there are innumerable ideas, feelings, and activities he may link to his own behavior. The particular ones he singles out may reflect his own general conception of evil. If he follows the precepts of Islam, he may attach the judgment of evil to thoughts and impulses not likely to be communicated to anyone; to actions that disturb others in a relatively trivial way; and to deeds that not only have serious consequences for the Victim or Victims but that also transgress the vital, moral rules of the group or the society.[48] Such a distinction between evil thoughts and evil behavior, though always intriguing, is never absolute because thoughts spill into action, and actions generate thoughts.

By and large, I suppose, the Judge is almost always tempted to judge himself by his actions rather than by his thoughts and dispositions. He may also recognize a solipsistically encased inner self and hence the possibility, rather the probability, of a discrepancy between what he does and what he feels. Were anyone on the outside acquainted with his feelings or motives, he confesses—to himself—that he might be judged evil. Should he be disturbed by such a discrepancy? Should he consider himself a hypocrite? And then in the West, if he is relatively well educated and sophisticated, he may have been affected by Freud and the master's disciples, as a result of which he gains or imagines he gains insight into himself from his night- or daydreams, from the slips of his own tongue, from selective perception and forgetting. Is he shocked by the disparity between the relative purity of his conscious thoughts and the impurity of the desires he discovers within himself, particularly in his own dreams? Should he consider himself evil because of those dreams, or should he extol himself because during waking life he has managed to suppress the impulses in behalf of nobler sentiments and actions? On a phenomenological level I suspect that self-judgment regarding responsibility is delayed until some sort of self-assessment has occurred. "I could not stop myself from doing it because . . ."—and the ending of the sentence depends upon the Judge's values, which are based, in turn, upon his society, the groups to which he refers his behavior, and his own experiences. If he feels, according to Hindu belief, that his status and actions result from his conduct in a previous existence, he may feel both less and more responsible for what he does here and now: His present conduct stems from a previous incarnation he has not controlled and in turn will affect him when and if he returns in a future incarnation.

It is conceivable, however, that the Judge may not hold himself responsible for what he does. He *may* apply to himself the same standards he employs in judging other persons,[49] although he *may* have a stronger tendency to ascribe his own behavior to factors "inherent in the situation" and the behavior of others to their own "stable dispositions."[50] On the other hand, he *may* call himself responsible if he has successfully achieved an objective and may ascribe a failure or a neutral outcome to other persons or to some aspect of the external situations.[51] If the last generalization is really valid, it could follow that an Evildoer who rejoices in his evildoing might call himself responsible, but if he has any regrets, he would then absolve himself.

Some aspects of behavior are perceived only by the individual himself. I am thinking particularly of falsehoods. "The lie," according to one philosopher, "is the specific evil which man has introduced into nature. . . . In a lie the spirit practices treason against itself."[52] One wonders whether all men everywhere either lie to themselves or to others and whether lying in behalf of some higher cause is ever justified. An even more elusive question is whether the Judge applies the same criteria concerning truth and falsehood to others as he does to himself. Silence ordinarily is considered harmless and is judged to be discreet or golden. But a philosopher asks whether Abraham was "ethically justified" in remaining silent in front of his son Isaac and his wife when God had commanded him to sacrifice the boy.[53] Abraham thus concealed an intention he judged good, and they probably would have called evil.

Ordinarily, I assume, the Judge who is awake believes—rightly or wrongly—that he controls what he does: he decides to raise his right hand, to drink water, to listen to music, or not to do so. Even a Muslim must assent to this feeling of free will with respect to simple actions when he states in the words of a devout but not necessarily typical follower of Mohammed that "it is indeed fantastic that a creature so hopelessly dependent upon the creation of God in the matter of accomplishing anything should claim to possess a will of his own."[54] At the other extreme, the Judge may be convinced, as one Western advocate of Theologic Man would have it, that ultimately he is responsible for himself because he is human and hence "capable of choosing between life and death and of preferring death if life can be preserved only at the price of submitting to unbearable conditions."[55] Such a Judge, however, may also recognize that environmental circumstances impose obvious limitations upon himself, and, when they do, he absolves himself of responsibility. He is not responsible for the fact that he is not a genius. He *may* experience, moreover, sudden feelings or impulses he finds difficult to explain, no less to attribute to himself.[56] He *may* believe, especially if they lead to evil, that such impulses spring not from himself but from some mischievous god, from an evil spirit, or from the malevolence of another person. Such a supernatural or superhuman explanation may relieve him of a feeling of responsibility, may impel him to evil, and may—as in Greek tragedy—instill guilt within himself afterward.[57] If he continues to commit evil deeds, he *may* no longer be able to distinguish the strain within himself. He does not pass self-judgment, he considers his deeds to be justified.[58]

An individual and an outside Judge may disagree concerning whether he is a Victim. In a laboratory situation, for example, the subject *may* feel that he is being treated unjustly if he is convinced that the ratio of his own satisfaction and effort is less than the corresponding ratio of someone else.[59] But the Judge, literally or figuratively, may not arrive at the same ratio.

Precepts abound enabling the Judge to absolve himself of responsibility and hence of evil. There are ready-made rationalizations: insults must be avenged, it is all right to strike back in self-defense, maniacs running amok must be shot. The same deceptions may be applied to other persons: he did not really mean to do it; he will never do it again; he must now live with himself and his conscience, hence I should not judge him to be an Evildoer. Projection is also possible: if I am good, then he must be too, for he is like me.

NOTES

1. John Whitney Hall, "Changing Conceptions of the Modernization of Japan," in Marius B. Jansen, ed., *Changing Japanese Attitudes toward Modernization* (Princeton: Princeton University Press, 1965), pp. 7-41.

2. Monica Blumenthal et al., *Justifying Violence* (Ann Arbor: Institute for Social Research, 1972), pp. 71-95.

3. Amaury de Riencourt, *Sex and Power in History* (New York: David McKay, 1974), pp. 162-63.

4. Mao Tse-tung, *An Anthology of His Writings* (New York: New American Library, 1971), p. 219.

5. Kahil Gibran, *The Prophet* (London: William Heinemann, 1926), pp. 61-63.

6. Ruth Nanda Anshen, "Thou shalt not . . . ," in Ruth Nanda Anshen, ed., *Moral Principles of Action* (New York: Harpers, 1952), pp. 3-38.

7. L. Cristiani, *Satan in the Modern World* (London: Barrie & Rockliff, 1959), pp. 67-69.

8. Liliane Frey-Rohn, "Evil from the Psychological Point of View," in Curatorium of the C. G. Jung Institute, *Evil* (Evanston: Northwestern University Press, 1967), pp. 121-50.

9. Dean Keith Simonton, "The Causal Relation Between War and Scientific Discovery," *Journal of Cross-Cultural Psychology* 7 (1976): 133-44.

10. Richard Cavendish, *The Powers of Evil* (New York: Putnam's, 1975), pp. 64-69.

11. Delmer M. Brown, *Nationalism in Japan* (Berkeley: University of California Press, 1955), p. 114.

12. Martin Buber, "The Suspension of Ethics," in Anshen, *Moral Principles,* pp. 223-27.

13. Søren Kierkegaard, *Fear and Trembling* (Princeton: Princeton University Press, 1968), pp. 64-65.

14. Leopold Schwarzschild, *The Red Prussian* (New York: Scribner's, 1947), p. 202.

15. Joseph H. Jackson, "Measurement of Ethical Values," *Perceptual and Motor Skills* 36 (1973): 1075-88.

16. Mahmoud A. Wahba, "Preferences among Alternative Forms of Equity," *Journal of Social Psychology* 87 (1972): 107-15.

17. James Garrett and William L. Lebby, "Role of Inequality in Mediating Responses to Inequity in the Dyad," *Journal of Personality and Social Psychology* 28 (1973): 21-27.

18. M. B. Ahern, *The Problem of Evil* (New York: Schocken Books, 1971), p. 18.

19. Marvin E. Shaw and Jefferson L. Sulzer, "An Empirical Test of Heider's Levels in Attribution of Responsibility," *Journal of Abnormal and Social Psychology* 69 (1964): 39-46.

20. R. Steven Schiavo, "Locus of Control and Judgments about Another's Accident," *Psychological Reports* 32 (1973): 483-88.

21. E. Jerry Phares and James Lamiell, "Internal-External Control, Interpersonal Judgments of Others in Need, and Attribution of Responsibility," *Journal of Personality*, 43 (1975): 23-38.

22. Bernard Berofsky, *Determinism* (Princeton: Princeton University Press, 1971), pp. 315-16.

23. Leonard W. Doob, *Public Opinion and Propaganda* (Hamden: Archon Books, 1966), pp. 245-50.

24. Philip P. Hallie, *The Paradox of Cruelty* (Middletown: Wesleyan University Press, 1969), p. 14.

25. Quoted in Frank Tannenbaum, *Slave and Citizen* (New York: Random House, 1946), p. 77.

26. Cf. Troy Duster, "Conditions for Guilt-Free Massacre," in Nevill Sanford et al., eds., *Sanctions for Evil* (San Francisco: Jossey-Bass, 1971), pp. 25-36.

27. Richard Hammer, *The Court-Martial of Lt. Calley* (New York: Coward, McCann, and Geoghegan, 1971), p. 4.

28. Herbert C. Kelman and Lee H. Lawrence, "Assignment of Responsibility in the Case of Lt. Calley," *Journal of Social Issues* 28, no. 1 (1972): 177-212.

29. Cathaleene Jones and Elliot Aronson, "Attribution of Fault to a Rape Victim as a Function of Respectability of the Victim," *Journal of Personality and Social Psychology* 26 (1973): 415-19.

30. Suresh Kanekar and Maharukh B. Kolsawalla, "The Relation of Respectability and Responsibility," *Journal of Social Psychology* 102 (1977): 183-88.

31. William Chase Greene, *Moira* (Cambridge: Harvard University Press, 1944), p. 4.

32. Riencourt, *Sex and Power*, pp. 91, 96.

33. E. E. Evans-Pritchard, *Nuer religion* (Oxford: Clarendon, 1956), pp. 17, 21, 189.

34. Joanne Joseph et al., "Perceived Aggression," *Journal of Social Psychology* 103 (1977):277-89. Also Marvin B. Scott and Stanford M. Lyman, "Accounts," *American Sociological Review* 33 (1968): 46-62.

35. Elaine Walster, "Assignment of Responsibility for an Accident," *Journal of Personality and Social Psychology* 3 (1966): 73-79.

36. Jerry I. Shaw and Paul Skolnick, "Attribution of Responsibility for a Happy Accident," *Journal of Personality and Social Psychology* 18 (1971): 380-83.

37. Air Marshall Sir Robert Saundby, cited by David Irving, *The Destruction of Dresden* (London: William Kimber, 1963), p. 5.

38. Ibid., p. 234.

39. Ibid., pp. 19, 43.

40. Ibid., p. 100.

41. Ibid., p. 136.

42. Ibid., pp. 142-43.

43. Edward M. Opton, Jr., "It Never Happened and Besides They Deserved It," in Sanford et al., *Sanctions*, pp. 49-70.

44. International Military Tribunal, *Trial of the Major War Criminals before the International Military Tribunal* (Nuremberg, 1947).

45. Melvin J. Lerner, "The Desire for Justice and Reactions to Victims," in J. Macaulay and L. Berkowitz, eds., *Altruism and Helping Behavior* (New York: Academic Press, 1970), pp. 205-29.

46. William Ryan, *Blaming the Victim* (New York: Pantheon, 1971), p. 81.

47. Marion L. Starkey, *The Devil in Massachusetts* (New York: Knopf, 1950), p. 248.

48. Sr. Muhammad Zafrullah Khan, "Moral Principles as the Basis of Islamic Culture," in Anshen, *Moral Principles*, pp. 559-77.

49. Richard E. Nisbett and Stuart Valins, "Perceiving the Causes of One's Own Behavior," in Edward E. Jones et al., *Attribution* (Morristown: General Learning Press, 1971), pp. 63-78.

50. Edward E. Jones and Richard E. Nisbett, "The Actor and the Observer," in Jones et al., *Attribution*, pp. 79-94.

51. Robert J. Wolosin, Steven J. Sherman, and Amnon Til, "Effects of Co-operation and Competition on Responsibility Attribution after Success and Failure," *Journal of Experimental Social Psychology* 9 (1973): 220-35.

52. Martin Buber, *Good and Evil* (New York: Scribner's, 1953), p. 7.

53. Kierkegaard, *Fear and Trembling*, pp. 81, 91.

54. H. M. Matin, *Determinism and Freedom* (Karachi: Marsh Publishing House, n.d.), p. 21.

55. Ludwin von Mises, *Theory and History* (New Haven: Yale University Press, 1957), p. 179.

56. E. R. Dodds, *The Greeks and the Irrational* (Berkeley: University of California Press, 1959), p. 14.

57. Greene, *Moira*, pp. 6-7.

58. John Dewey, *Human Nature and Conduct* (New York: Modern Library, 1922), p. 211.

59. J. Stacy Adams, "Inequity in Social Exchange," *Advances in Experimental Psychology* 2 (1965): 267-99.

Part Three

EVILDOERS

7

CAUSATION: EVILDOERS

Why does evil exist? Why are some persons Evildoers and others not? Under what circumstances is evil committed? These are the eternal questions which must now torment us. The emphasis is completely upon human beings, although it is recognized again that there are situations—such as a tornado—in which there are ostensibly no Evildoers, only Victims. The qualification "ostensibly" is required because, although persons have no more control over winds than they do over tides or sunspots, they may ultimately be found to play some role in producing the evil—for example, through the changes they introduce into man's habitat as a result of pollution or other environmental changes.

Causation in the affairs of men is seldom easy to establish unless a well-controlled experiment can be performed—and even then problems of sampling the human race arise. We must be content with tentative hypotheses concerning cause-and-effect sequences. A given sequence may be contingent upon circumstances, and hence we cannot "deny that it is the necessary outcome of the preceding state of affairs" rather, "it means we mortal men do not know whether or not it will happen."[1] Thus we can be certain only—and then by definition—that some Judge will consider the person in his society who breaks a taboo to be an Evildoer. The problem is to discover why the taboo is broken. Why are there individuals who steal, rape, loot, murder, deceive, fornicate, wage war? We may say that men steal when they are hungry, and they may be hungry during a recession if they are unemployed and welfare benefits are insufficient. But not all hungry men steal, and not all men are hungry under these conditions. The cause-and-effect sequence, therefore, is elusive.

The actual or alleged Evildoer, moreover, is not always easy to locate. We can point with assurance to the murderer of an innocent Victim as an Evildoer if he has been convicted during a completely "fair" trial. Is the adolescent who commits murder while mugging a victim responsible for his action if he comes from a slum area and a broken family? What shall we say of the many Evildoers who have some responsibility, direct or indirect, for modern warfare?

Should the historian of a society be judged an unintentional Evildoer? Men almost always have an interest in their past; they wish to know how human beings, their own group, or they themselves have come into existence. Everywhere, therefore, oral traditions are transmitted from generation to generation, and in the modern world professionals are charged with the responsibility of presenting the past as accurately as possible. No trace of evildoing here—perhaps. But some Judges, as well as historians, know that usually too many facts in the past must be collated and that a historian must be selective if he is to be intelligible. Modern statesmen, especially those in Europe during the last century, have wished the teaching of history "to bring about deeper under-standing of the righteousness of the existing political situation and greater loyalty to the rulers of the state";[2] and the same wish can usually be found among members of school boards and among officials who select textbooks. Some Judges, including historians, believe that the teaching of nationalism eventually leads to the evil of war as a consequence. But children, they also say, should appreciate their heritage, a cherishable value and also one inducing them to defend their country when its leaders take them into a war. The historians may very well be devoted professionally to their craft and may themselves abhor the evil consequence of what they write. Are they, I ask again, Evildoers?

If it is true that the intention of any human being is usually difficult to determine, largely because of the care we must exercise as a result of the insight provided by Freud and to the many puzzles mentioned in the previous chapter, the search is compounded many times in our surveys and evaluations of organizations: who are the Evildoers? It is so easy or glib to say that society is responsible for some aspect of evil; but that concept begs the question by not identifying in the past or present the actual persons responsible for the wrong decisions or the evil acts—and they may never be discoverable.[3] Even when Evildoers can be specified, perplexities remain. During the late 1960s in the United States, for example, many of the crusaders in favor of civil rights believed in nonviolence, since violence alwavs has evil consequences. The marches they organized in behalf of their principles are said to have "elicited some of the official violence which outsiders had been ignoring and caused it to be displayed on television."[4] Perhaps, then, the end result was a blow against violence in general or this particular utilization of violence as a result of the exposure on a mass medium. And so there was a string of events: nonviolent marchers, provocation of violence, perhaps condemnation of violence. In addition, it is not inconceivable that some of the organizers of the marches had anticipated—intended—the very effect that was achieved. Who, then, were the Evildoers: the provocateurs, the provoked, or the allegedly indifferent public?

On a comparatively descriptive level, as has been indicated in the previous chapter, a Judge probably considers an individual an Evildoer when, after being confronted with alternatives, he does not behave like a Theologic Man and makes the "wrong" choice. The wrong choice is then said to be the cause of the evildoing. Here is one of the most fundamental contentions of Christian theology, as well as of philosophical thinking. Adam and Eve ate of the tree of knowledge and henceforth must have known the difference between right and wrong, a differentiation that only God previously knew.[5] Presumed once more is free will: "God created beings possessed of free will in order that they might be in a position to acquire merit by acting rightly *when it was possible for them to act wrongly.*" From this it follows that if human beings "are to be free to choose wrongly . . . , some wrong choices will almost certainly be made" and hence "evil must always be present in the universe in order that it may be chosen."[6] In the words of St. Paul concisely expressed in Latin: "Video meliora proboque; deteriora sequor" ("For the good that I would do I do not; but the evil which I would not, that I do").[7] When an individual breaks the taboos of a society and hence is judged to be an Evildoer on the basis of the social-moral criterion of evil or when it is asserted that "man's true enemy is within himself" and that this enemy "lies in the strength of his own uncontrolled passions and appetites," the presumption is that the true cause of the wrong choice resides within the Evildoer himself.[8] "Intentional freedom," according to an anthropologist, "is said to be the defining characteristic of man and refers to the human capacity to form an intention and to seek to realize it in action."[9]

Why, then, does an individual make the wrong choice and thus become an Evildoer? That is the scientific, not the theological, question. He may not in fact be acquainted with the alternatives postulated by the theologians. He may not be aware that the alternative he selects is the evil one as judged by someone inside or outside his own society. This state of affairs exists especially if he is prejudiced or ethnocentric: what others call evil, he considers normal and good. He may have a different set of values or perceive the situation quite differently. The man he has murdered or swindled he believes to have been an Evildoer, and hence his own deed is a justifiable reprisal; he may thus delude himself into believing that he has accomplished good.[10] In other instances he might agree that his actions have evil consequences if those consequences were made known to him. He has little or no information, for example, concerning the ways in which a bank uses the money he deposits in his savings account; he might believe that some of the bank's investments are quite evil because they support industries contributing to the environment's pollution.

Existentially, even on a hypothetical level, it is often most difficult to choose between two alternatives: which one is good, which one evil? "Should one risk one's life," a student of ethics asks, "to help a man who is a) drowning, b) trapped in a fire, c) stepping in front of a speeding truck, d) hanging by his fingernails over an abyss?" The reply: "Only a lack of self-esteem would permit one to value one's life no higher than that of any random stranger."[11] Self-esteem is perhaps always a good value, but should one let the man die in order not to risk one's own life? If the stranger perishes, would the bystander thereafter judge himself to be selfish and an Evildoer? A devout Christian might say that we should rescue the stranger, whether he turns out to be a good man or a rascal, in order to set a good example for mankind: we are interdependent and cannot overlook our responsibilities. In broader terms, can evil ever be avoided when one is selfish? Are one's actions always good when one is selfless?

The person judged to be an Evildoer may claim that extenuating circumstances forced him to make a wrong decision or one that he would not have made under other circumstances. A writer absolutely opposed to war has admitted: "For my part, I would not hesitate to use force to restrain a mad dog or a mad man."[12] In a more complicated, nonhypothetical illustration, most subjects in a series of experiments did not hesitate to give what they believed to be severe electric shocks to another human being (actually he was not shocked but, being a confederate of the investigator, acted as though he had been) when instructed to do so as part of what they had been told was a scientific experiment. Such cruel—and evil?—behavior, according to the experimenter's findings, was facilitated by the fact that the "ordinary person" felt a sense of obligation to the experimenter and believed he should behave like a good subject. He became absorbed in performing as he had been instructed, he did not consider himself responsible for the setup in which he was participating, he shifted from moral considerations to concentrating upon his own performance, and he felt he was simply obeying when, as he hesitated to increase the strength of the alleged shock he was giving the "suffering" Victim, he was told to "continue" to carry on.[13] These experiments have been well publicized, and many persons have been deeply disturbed by them. Why? Perhaps because they do not wish to acknowledge the thin line separating good from evil behavior, a line that may exist within themselves. Perhaps they fear that they also can become Evildoers too easily by inventing good, plausible reasons for their own actions.

So far the analysis has been only descriptive, but now the questions must be raised: Why does the Evildoer make the wrong choice? Why is he unaware that the choice is evil? Why does he find extenuating circumstances enabling him to make that choice? The first explanation is almost self-evident: he is defective in some respect and hence, as suggested in connection with the Judge's opinion concerning his responsibility, he is unable to choose the superior path. Reference has been made to children who have not yet learned the principles of morality prevailing in their society; to imbeciles, morons, and the insane; to persons under the influence of drugs or extraordinary emotions. These genetic, physiological, or momentary conditions are considered to be the cause of the evildoing. The behavior of such persons is no more purposive, it has been said, than someone with a severe brain tumor can be said to be responsible for his choice of alternative actions.[14] Similarly, it is asserted that many of those individuals engaging in taboo breaking, serious antisocial behavior—so-called sociopaths—*may* suffer from a "defective quality" with respect to interpersonal relations: they lack "the capacity for identification with others," they identify "in only limited or circumscribed ways," or their identifications are "shifting or transient."[15] Care must be exercised, however, in the use of this explanation. The physical and sexual abuse of children in American society is reported to be "usually not inflicted by mentally ill or pathological parents." Although some pathology may be involved, this form of what is almost always judged to be evil is rather "the logical outgrowth of our cultural heritage and predilection toward violence."[16]

The inability to make the distinction between good and evil may also reflect the resilience of Evildoers. Like addicts, they may begin to assume that their evil actions are part of the normal state of affairs. They retain their peace of mind by indulging in evil again and again. Fatalism sets in: so it is, I cannot do otherwise. Evil turns into good, or at least it is so judged, particularly when there is positive support from one's associates. Evildoing may generalize, cruelty in one sphere may transfer to other spheres. The Evildoer, as a series of Hogarth's drawings suggests, *may* begin by torturing animals and end by maiming a human being.[17]

In addition, I think we approach an explanation of evildoing more closely when we agree with the contention of a psychoanalyst that "some people have no freedom to choose the good because their character structure has lost the capacity to act in acordance with the good."[18] This "character" can be analyzed in terms of the beliefs and the personality traits apparently related to evildoing. It should be obvious, moreover, that both the beliefs and the traits result from the way individuals have been socialized during their childhood. In fact, virtually every relevant study establishes the probability that there are "child-rearing antecedents of moral development."[19] Equally obvious is the fact that then and later in life some moral standards "may be acquired deliberately" and "unintentionally or even without awareness."[20]

On a piecemeal basis, an attempt can be made to delineate factors associated with the "wrong" choice. First, let us turn to beliefs or belief systems. A novelist is reported to have written that "human beings only started to fight each other in earnest when there was no longer anything to fight about."[21] The "anything to fight about" must refer to the basic requirements of living—such as food and shelter—which may be viewed in terms of sheer animal existence because above that level there is much to produce conflict, especially in the realm of those beliefs concerning what constitutes the good life and its attainment. Like many other peoples, Iranians are reported to be very conscious of their long and varied history, and therefore they believe they must defend their culture at all costs. These beliefs in turn produce policies and actions that may or may not be judged good by outsiders.[22]

A belief in a particular theology affects whether the individual becomes an Evildoer. From one Christian standpoint, evil arises when a person does not accept the view that "the finiteness, dependence, and the insufficiency of man's mortal life are facts which belong to God's plan of creation and must be accepted with reverence and humility" and instead seeks "to comprehend the whole" or "to realize it."[23] Christians—and others too—may be convinced that they themselves have no or little responsibility for the evil they would or do commit because they believe they have been tempted by forces beyond themselves[24] or, when those forces are personified, by the Devil himself who thus functions as an overpowering scapegoat.[25]

Society or particular groups can supply the convictions enabling individuals to overcome the inhibitions learned during childhood and to become Evildoers. Except perhaps among mercenaries, soldiers may not be able to fight effectively unless they believe their cause is just and that of the enemy unjust. The morale of American combat crews in World War II, for example, tended to be high when they were acquainted with and sympathetic toward U.S. aims.[26] Both sides in America's Civil War believed they were defending noble objectives: the South, its labor system and its "entire way of life"; the North, saving the Union and democracy.[27] Clearly ideologies may support a good as well as an evil cause, and therefore the challenge is to select the former and reject the latter. But now can the decision be made?

On the basis of experience, an individual may acquire his own idiosyncratic beliefs that lead him to engage in what is judged to be evil behavior. Evil appears everywhere; why should he not share in the spoils? From the very beginning, there have been evil men and evil deeds: he has good precedents to follow. Punishment is unlikely; even if he is caught, others will also be caught, and surely it will be impossible or impractical to punish everybody. Or he believes himself different from his peers: they, not he, are capable of evil; they, not he, will be punished if apprehended. If he is a nonbeliever, ostensibly he does not fear everlasting fire or his next incarnation because he assumes neither exists. The breaking of a taboo or a principle is just a formality, why worry? He may merely be curious: Does the fruit have an exotic taste? Why not try it? Will the heavens really tumble if I commit this sin just once or twice?

Researchers must often search in vain when they try to discover a relation between beliefs and activities usually considered evil or semievil. No relation, for example, *may* exist between the values of civilian and criminal samples and their proclivity toward violence.[28] But the measuring instruments may be at fault. Violence for the civilians has been measured by means of three contingency questions, for the criminals by means of an objective measure (the type of crime for which they had been committed).

And now: the personality traits associated with evildoing. I hold the view, call it optimistic or cynical, that at least on a paper-and-pencil level, the one on which most psychological investigations of this kind tend to be conducted, there is likely to be some relation, however minute, between an abstract conception of evil and almost any personality trait so measured. I would guess, for example, that, with the possible exception of anger, all the other classical deadly sins—covetousness, envy, gluttony, lust, pride, and sloth—reflect enduring personality tendencies and hence are likely to give rise to evil in some form. But I am uncertain which of the four classical temperaments (phlegmatic, choleric, melancholic, sanguine) is more likely to produce persons inclined to become Evildoers.

I have two candidates for traits that seem to incline persons to commit evil deeds. The first is the absence of self-mastery. The inability to control one's own impulses makes the individual less inclined to choose wisely between alternatives and to reflect upon the consequences of what he does and then to pass secondary judgments. The second is closely related to the first: impatience. Impatience leads to impulsiveness and recklessness. Thus there is "the assumption current in all modern legal systems that intent to do wrong is necessary for the commission of a crime."[29] Without premeditation, again a guess, reckless impatience prevents the individual from drawing upon all the intellectual and emotional resources of which he is capable. I further assume without evidence that some persons are more impatient than others. "Think before you act," "count to ten before you reply," the platitudes state; and yet to Confucius may be attributed (out of context from the rest of his philosophy) the definition of "a proper man" as one who "acts first and then his talk fits what he has done."[30]

One thousand high Nazi prisoners of war were interviewed between 1942 and 1944 and, according to a psychiatrist, the following eight attributes characterized the syndrome that they shared and that apparently facilitated the perpetration of the evil acts associated with their regime:

1. gottgläubig [believing in God] or else a nihilistic atheist
2. unresolved bond with an internalized father-figure colouring several of his other significant traits
3. dearth of deep positive relations to maternal figures and attitudes
4. heightened intolerance of tenderness with a tendency to despise and deride it
5. cult of manliness . . . homosexuality
6. preponderance of "anti-social" sadism
7. the tendency to project and see hostile intent outside the self, thus readily feeling persecuted, discriminated against or unjustly hated
8. neurotic anxiety[31]

Although roughly the same syndrome was found when eight "SS killers" were more carefully examined psychiatrically, at least two caveats must be entered concerning the postulated traits. In the first place, the syndrome alone does not account for their evil or cruelty; other factors must also be taken into account. In addition, each individual, though he exemplified the syndrome to some degree, also was more or less unique in some respects. Of one of the eight, for example, it is said that "the longing for a good father to deliver him from inimical forces all around him runs like a red thread through his whole life story"—and such a thread was not that clear in connection with the other seven.[32]

The illustrations about to be given from the paper-and-pencil approach are meant to be suggestive only. A favorite trait being measured during the last decade or so, to which reference has been previously made, has been called "locus of control": a distinction is drawn between individuals believing their destiny stems largely from outside forces (external control) and those convinced they are masters of their fate (internal control).[33] According to one capable summary of the research, there *may* be a tendency for those believing in internal control, in contrast with those ascribing their fate to externalities, to:

1. withstand pressures directing them to behave in a certain circumscribed manner.
2. know more about what is important to them and [to] seem more eager to gain information that would help increase their probabilities for successful experiences.
3. [achieve more as measured by] grade-point average, achievement test scores, and school room achievement among gradeschool children.
4. take action to confront their difficulties.
5. [come from] a warm, accepting home with predictable, consistent standards [at least as reported by] children and adolescents . . . though expressions of parental attitudes about the same elements seem unrelated to the child's locus of control.
6. [have learned] successfully [to] cope with immediate difficulties.[34]

It could be argued that each of these half-dozen generalizations connotes better "adjustment" to the immediate milieu and to society in general, and hence that persons subscribing to an internal rather than an external view of control are less evil prone. But there are difficulties with this suggestion. Under some circumstances, the very attributes listed above conceivably can have the reverse effect. The first one, for example—withstanding outside pressures—may induce a nonconforming attitude, which might mean taboo breaking and hence evildoing rather than a better or healthier adaptation. Then, most but not all the investigations have employed American college students as subjects, and very often the variable with which the locus-of-control variable has been correlated is also a paper-and-pencil score. Indeed, the writer on whose summary the six generalizations are based indicates that "at least nine different" paper-and-pencil tests have been employed to measure the control variable, and one investigator warns that those subjects or patients attributing control to external forces may in some instances be using that explanation as "a verbal technique of defense" or rationalization.[35] Moreover, the generalizations being derived from literally hundreds of studies are not as clear-cut as they appear in the above summary: contradictory results have been obtained;

the relations from a statistical viewpoint—although they could not have arisen by chance and hence must be considered significant in this limited sense—are generally low; and in at least one instance locus of control was unrelated to what might be called evildoing (allegedly shocking a laboratory victim).[36]

In spite of these deficiencies and uncertainties, the research on locus of control cannot be tossed aside as part of a faddish scientific zeitgeist that eventually will fade into obscurity. For one thing, there is commonsense validity to the finding that in American society blacks and other underprivileged groups *may* be more inclined to believe their decisions originate in external rather than internal circumstances.[37] This is what one should expect from persons whose lives tend to be controlled by others. Then, there *may* be—occasionally but not always[38]—low but significant relations between this locus-of-control variable and political activity or interest in politics,[39] although the direction of the connection with liberalism or conservatism is quite unclear.[40] Finally, almost every study casts a broad hint that the belief one has concerning locus of control *may* be related to some other attribute—I am thinking particularly of alienation[41]—facilitating victim proneness in our society. No nirvana can be attained by proselytizing in behalf of this particular belief, maybe just a glimpse or two.

Speculation continues. A series of investigations indicates that some Americans *may* be more dependent on external conditions as they perceive and adjust themselves to their physical and social environment than others. Correlated with such "field dependence" are traits that may possibly influence evildoing or eviljudging. Those less field dependent or analytic, for example, *may* have a greater "sense of separate identity," which manifests itself in a "limited need for guidance and support from others; ability to establish and, within limits, maintain attitudes, judgments, sentiments without continuous reference to external standards; a stable self-view, despite variations in social context."[42] Could it be that such persons are less evil prone since they are not so susceptible to outside influences that might tempt them to become Evildoers or—to adopt the contrary stance—more evil prone for exactly the opposite reason? We find no answer to this double-barreled question when we examine the children of mothers who have apparently fostered or inhibited their differentiation, for the children's "adjustment" appears to have been helped or hindered by either emphasis. Then, too,

"adjustment" as such brings us no closer to the problem of evil proneness, inasmuch as this vague concept does not suggest whether the
person or situation, to which adjustment or nonadjustment is made,
implies evildoing or the reverse.

Other specific research indicates that there *may* be a relation between
children's sensitivity with respect to judging emotions and their willingness to be altruistic, so that possibly evildoing may require insensi-
tivity.[43] That such a generalization is either limited in scope or of doubtful
validity, however, is suggested by the observation that, although dis-
agreement may be diminished, "altruistic behavior between political
actors is not, in general, sufficient to remove areas of contention between
actors."[44] Perhaps altruism as such does not diminish conflict, always
potentially a source of evil. "Humanism," possibly a trait that opposes
evildoing, *may* affect the individual's tendency to follow ideological
principles in determining his decision, to adopt less self-centered and
more legalistic and principle-oriented standards, or to be more tolerant.[45]
In general, although we may say with mild conviction that antisocial
behavior is related to the individual's moral development, it seems
evident that more than a single trait *may* be involved in evildoing and
that therefore this approach to our problem yields once more only a
scanty return.[46]

A more promising point of departure than traits is to consider the
individual's motivation tempting or compelling him to behave in an evil
manner. Any intellectual attempt to try to reduce that motivation to a
single drive is dramatic and impressive. Thus "the root causes of
human evil" are said to be "man's natural and inevitable urge to deny
mortality and achieve a heroic self-image."[47] Unquestionably this thesis
provides considerable insight into many instances of evil, such as the
cruelties in which men engage in order to try to gain heavenly bliss or
the accumulation of exaggerated wealth in order to leave behind concrete reminders of their accomplishments. In spite of its face validity,
however, the analysis is too sweeping; it is like saying that war or murder has only a single cause when we know that there are numerous ones.
To reduce all the causes to one source, however abstract or inviting, is
too much of a simplification.

We must take into account, therefore, other motives that operate
either simultaneously or independently.[48] Whenever a human being
fails to achieve a goal, no matter whether it be significant or trivial, he is

frustrated and is likely—but not always—to be aggressive. Thus aggression may result from the frustration of inevitable death, as just indicated, or from the frustration of losing one's job or being insulted by a friend. In discussing the relation of frustration and aggression, I have already indicated that the frustrated person *may* be aggressive, but it is not absolutely certain that he will be; he may also be constructive. Being aggressive, however, may mean that actually or in fantasy, intentionally or unintentionally, he would hurt or harm others (or their surrogate) who thus perhaps become Victims. Reinterpreted slightly, St. Thomas's statement that "if we were completely free from natural limitations and hindrances of all sorts, we could not deliberately choose evil"[49] would suggest that, without frustrations resulting from a genetic constitution and a restrictive environment, taboos might not be broken and Theologic Man would be in a more advantageous position to select a good rather than an evil course of action.

If the frustrated person submerges the resulting aggression in fantasy, he will not victimize another individual. He has available, however, a host of aggressive outlets ranging from physical attack upon the presumed frustrator to some form of masochism when he considers himself the source of the frustration. That he can become an Evildoer is suggested by the possibility that he *may* find it rewarding to have the frustrator subjected to a painful experience.[50] Criminal actions and other forms of taboo breaking often result from failure to attain a desirable goal.

Gaining or retaining power is another reason why some persons become Evildoers, and they find the power gratifying in itself or because of the rewards it seems to bring. *Perhaps* the feeling of powerlessness produces neurotic or even psychotic tendencies.[51] If this be so, it is little wonder that some men "will fight to the death to protect the models of power on which their lives are predicated."[52] Then for various reasons the powerful person controls other persons and thus can easily become an Evildoer by making them his Victims: he occupies a position in government; he has prestige (as an expert, an authority, the recipient of respect or admiration as a result of past performance); he is a parent and hence can affect almost all aspects of a child's existence; he is a child and thus causes his parents to be forever anxious concerning their responsibilities toward him or to feel guilty concerning their failures in rearing him; he dominates the Victim who is his captive in prison or in war. The bombardier who drops bombs or poison upon enemy territory in a very literal sense has power over the physical forces affecting the Victims beneath. Whether "ethics is the way the weak limit the strong, not simply the way the strong philosophize amongst themselves" is a question I leave to the professional philosophers, with the expectation that most of them (the non-Marxians, at any rate) will maintain that they are objective and relatively unaffected by the pressures from their own societies.[53]

Second, it may be true that many individuals have a "secret love of violence,"[54] which, if violence in general or in particular forms be considered evil producing, makes them prone to become Evildoers. Sadism, consequently, may be the conscious or unconscious motive behind evil, and so in everyday life one can point to riots, other forms of mob action, and the deliberate destruction of other persons or their property.[55] Sadism, we know, implies masochism, and more than a generation ago a psychoanalyst suggested that "however much you preach to nationalists that it does not pay to cut off one's nose to spite someone else's face, the lesson cannot be learned so long as unconscious masochism remains an unknown and unmeasured quantity."[56] Whether "unconscious masochism" produces an eagerness or at least a willingness to participate in wars is less important than the contention that preaching and even educating will not make men less prone to fight.

And so it appears that there are persons whose evildoing results not from situations, beliefs, or traits but from the desire to commit evil. Evil brings them satisfaction. Psychopaths and sociopaths presumably have such strong antisocial grudges that they orient their existence around evildoing. They may be sadists wishing to do harm or masochists hoping unconsciously that evildoing will bring them punishment. But their behavior is not in fact completely consistent. A habitual thief steals only from certain kinds of persons; he may also be religious and not even tempted to walk off with a holy chalice from a church, though I must add that some chalices mysteriously disappear.

The appalling observation to make at this point is that apparently everywhere there are some persons capable of torture and cruelty. Again and again in the modern world of the West we hear of the suffering of defenseless persons. We can say that they are the product of a more or less unique development in a particular kind of society, yet the universality of evildoing and the methods employed are depressingly striking. The Evildoers must bring pain: physical pain on the skin, the genitals, the breasts, the fingernails and toenails, or psychic pain through humiliation, anxiety, deprivation. They know what they themselves would avoid, and this they inflict upon others. The very reflective capacity of human beings, therefore, gives rise to evildoing in its most terrifying form.

According to proverbial lore, evil is said to be more attractive than good and hence either constitutes a goal in its own right or else enables the Evildoer to attain his various goals. Faust sold his soul to the Devil not only to achieve beauty but also for the sake of earthly pleasures, most or many of which he knew to be evil. The thief steals because in desperation he wishes to enjoy what he obtains. Pornography is ancient and ever popular. The lore may be wrong, for resisting temptation to break a taboo may require a strong conscience, but breaking the taboo may demand the circumvention of guilt—and we know that sometimes men and women must have pressure exerted upon them by other persons before they will engage in evil actions. Perhaps the traditional view that evil is easily perpetuated persists at least in Western society in order to discourage evil behavior; emphasizing its ease implies that an Evildoer has a weak character.

Whether or not the Evildoer enjoys or suffers from the evil he commits is too broad a question to be decided once and for all time. Did Pontius Pilate have any sincere or profound regrets concerning his debatable role in the crucifixion; Nero concerning his alleged responsibility for the burning of Rome; the English concerning the burning of Jeanne d'Arc; Cromwell concerning his treatment of the Irish; the American pioneers and their government concerning the slaughter of native Indians; Hitler concerning the "final solution" for the Jews; Russian (or German?) authorities concerning the massacre of Polish officers at Katyn; Nixon concerning the perverted morals and standards of his conduct as president?[57] Perhaps these Evildoers did rejoice, for them evil was rewarding and gratifying. One may speculate that they must have had regrets, pangs of conscience, or at least conflicting emotions as they contemplated or reviewed their misdeeds. Intimate knowledge of this sort, however, is not likely to be available: the Evildoers can conceal their feelings from outsiders and from themselves. Since the men I just mentioned were not half-witted, they must have been aware of the actual or potential judgments of some of their peers stemming from societal norms and hence they must have had—well, perhaps—a sense of guilt or misgiving if not regret. There must have been some trace of a conflict within them between impulses toward evil and good.

Another way to try to isolate the psychological and social factors associated with evil has the advantage of considering many factors simultaneously, and that is the cross-cultural approach, which, however, is largely statistical in nature. Let us assume, for example, that bellicosity is evil and that bellicose societies contain many Evildoers. A society is termed bellicose when "the majority of adult males are said to spend most of their daily life engaged in or preparing for war, raids, or homicidal vendettas"; when "the tribe is feared by surrounding tribes as an aggressor"; or when an ethnographer simply states that the tribe is "currently belligerent or warlike." In contrast, one is called low in bellicosity when none of the criteria just mentioned are satisfied; when war is "defined as waged primarily in revenge, or defensively, in response to the presence of warlike neighbors"; when the tribe is described as "peaceful, meek, friendly, non-aggressive, etc."; or when "war, raids, vendettas, etc. are said to be absent." In contrast with the societies where bellicosity so defined is "moderate or negligible," those in which it is "extreme" *tend* to be different with respect to certain practices and traits indicated below (the first figure in the parentheses is the number of societies on which the generalization is based, and the second is the degree of association between bellicosity and the variable, a figure that can range in theory from 0—no relation—to 1.00—a perfect relation):

1. *Childhood Practices*
   mother-son sleeping arrangements having a duration of one year or longer (33; .50)

   emphasis on development of self-reliance (52; .36)

   emphasis on development of achievement behavior (44; .36)

   complete or partial segregation of adolescent boys (69; .30)

2. *Personality Traits*
   high narcissism (87; .43)

   extreme sensitivity to insult (85; .24)

   extreme boastfulness (86; .37)

   strong or moderate emphasis on military glory (83; .72)

3. *Sexual Activities*

    premarital sexual activity not rare and weakly punished or freely permitted; or punished only if pregnancy resulted (67; .22)

    extramarital coitus punished (43; .49)

    obtaining of wives by difficult means (for example, bride price or exchanging of female relative) (87; .22)

    common or occasional polygamous marriages (85; .27)

4. *Social Institutions*

    achievement of political integration by a state rather than by the community or family (76; .29)

    strong or moderate emphasis on killing, torturing, or mutilating the enemy (82; .58)[58]

Innumerable other traits and practices have no significant association with bellicosity, however, and the above associations, with few exceptions, tend to be weak (as shown by the second figure in the parentheses). We have, nevertheless, at least the wisp of a suggestion that bellicosity is related to various kinds of behavior and institutions.

The final set of factors inducing evil is essentially social in nature: momentary or enduring pressures facilitating or requiring evil behavior. These factors cannot be disentangled from one another, but it seems clear that they have the potentiality of being influential. It is unnecessary to belabor the fact that parents exert an enormous influence on their children. In modern societies, the mass media are often accused of promoting evil, for example, by featuring violence. Should they in fact be condemned for displaying violence, or are their publics responsible because they crave and respond enthusiastically to such displays? As a matter of somewhat convincing fact, studies of American television that have attempted to show whether the violence of programs simply reflects the violence in American society or promotes such violence are, on the whole, inconclusive; the interpretation can go either way.[59]

Just as the heat of passion or a drug can have a momentary effect upon the individual and induce him to become an Evildoer, so the presence of other persons may have a similar effect. If not helping a Victim in apparent distress may be considered a form of evil, then *perhaps* the individual will be more evil prone in the presence than in the absence of another person who ignores the distress; and this social effect may be even stronger when he believes that the nonreactive bystander is similar rather than dissimilar to himself.[60] The size of the group affecting the Evildoer may vary from the scores of persons composing a crowd or mob to the handful constituting a committee, but in either situation the tendency to engage in group thinking or group action can be over-whelming.[61] This kind of social atmosphere may endure for long periods of time. The men who planned the raids on Dresden toward the end of World War II had grown accustomed to the bombing of civilian targets because English towns and cities had been devastated by the Germans, and the British themselves had been attacking Germany; more specifically, the type of fire storm created in Dresden had already been produced in the city of Hamburg.[62] Of even longer duration are the groups to which the individuals refer their behavior, and some of these, like gangs, may have norms promoting evil.[63] In one American penitentiary the prison guards formed an in-group of their own; they were more or less isolated from the rest of the surrounding community because they had separate living quarters, and they are reported to have developed "a psychological need to perceive prisoners as unchanging, lest the evil attributes they were felt to contain be released," as a result of which their own behavior toward these men might well be evaluated as evil by outside Judges.[64] Within the more enduring groups, the beliefs and attitudes that are the prerequisites to evildoing must usually be taught and learned. During the Nazi era those in control of concentration camps were given forced and sometimes painful lessons in cruelty by those who had already mastered the art before they were allowed or able to function on their own.[65] Rationalization through projection may be provided: they were going to attack me, and so I attacked first.[66] A tribe or a nation has different sets of values for its own members and for outsiders:[67] a kinsman may not be murdered, but an enemy of one's country during a war must be killed. A life is lost in both instances, but the judgments differ.

Sometimes, as in a boxing match or a duel, the individual seeks deliberately to harm or destroy his opponent in a face-to-face situation. Even then, however, it may be additionally necessary to hate the adversary; otherwise the tendency to break the taboo against harming or destroying another human being, so heavily reinforced during socialization and thereafter, inhibits evildoing. The engineering of hatred may not be easy to accomplish, yet all societies seem able to produce persons sufficiently expert to achieve that end. One's enemies, it is said, "must be depicted as subhuman, bestial, and unworthy of basic rights and privileges."[68] Experimental evidence gathered from American college students in our times *may* substantiate an observation of Tacitus that is probably also applicable to Evildoers before they create Victims: "It is a principle of human nature to hate those whom you have injured."[69] In the German prison camps the prisoners were often systematically degraded; even those suffering from diarrhea or dysentery were provided with insufficient or, in effect, no toilet facilities so that they often were compelled to defecate or urinate in their clothes or upon others nearby. They frequently lived amid the filth of their own excrement, urine, and vomit. The aim of this policy was not only the "complete humiliation and debasement" of the inmates and to reduce them to the status of children but to make it "easier for the SS to do their job." Thus "mass murder [could become] less terrible to the murderers, because the victims appeared less than human."[70] Interviews with SS officers after World War II also reveal that they themselves fostered beliefs justifying their own actions. They came to believe, for example, that the Victims had committed misdemeanors or were displaying hostility; hence, they deserved to be punished or killed.[71]

In order to injure and especially to kill a Victim, the potential Evildoer may do more than degrade that other person or project his own beliefs; he may try to make him into a nonperson.[72] This process has been called—because psychologists are addicted to fancy terms which, they hope, will render them famous or immortal—*deindividuation* or, from the standpoint of the Victim, *dehumanization*.[73] The obvious but tragic illustration is provided by warfare in which the armed forces fire a cannon or mortar from afar or drop bombs from the sky when the human beings thus killed or wounded are not visible. In simulated laboratory settings, such deindividuation *may* not be necessary to stimulate mild aggression, but the generalizability of this possibility seems most limited.[74]

As important as derogating or concealing the potential Victim is the removal of a feeling of responsibility from the potential or actual Evildoer. As evidence, young women in an American college participated in an experiment similar to the ones described earlier in this chapter: they delivered what they believed to be electric shocks to apparently disobedient subjects. The shocks were ostensibly stronger when these women were hooded than when they were not.[75] Although other interpretations are possible, there *may* be a strong tendency for warriors from societies that engage in "killing, torturing, or mutilating the enemy" to achieve "a feeling of anonymity" by changing their appearance before battle. They paint their bodies or face, they wear special garments, or they don masks; they do this, moreover, not to protect themselves or to display a symbol of status.[76] In Western and other societies, convicts, traitors, spies, or heroic dissenters are killed not by a single marksman but by a firing squad. In this connection it is interesting to note that official executioners, the men charged with hanging, garrotting, or electrocuting specific persons, themselves sometimes wear masks or, more generally, are hidden from their victims. In addition, they have "never" been "esteemed" figures in Western society, for apparently the idea of even legalized killing is repellent. Appreciating their own status, they have been driven to try to escape criticism through excessive drinking or even through suicide; or they have sought to gain some prestige by inventing ways to make their prescribed mode of killing more humane.[77] Apparently legal killers who have the final responsibility for the killing are not easily tolerated by those employing them and by themselves. The Nazi leaders, the ones who made the decisions concerning concentration camps, tried to remain "good people": they were far removed from those actually carrying out the work of executing the so-called enemies of the state.[78]

An Evildoer can appraise his own responsibility for a good or an evil action only within the framework of the freedom to select alternatives that he actually has or that he believes he has. It is clear, as one anthropologist has indicated, that there are "limitations imposed on individual or group activity in the major types of institutions which must exist if the society is to survive at all."[79] The individual, consequently, is absolved of responsibility in some situations in which restrictions upon him are imposed. May a soldier in the army disobey his commanding officer? May a young child disobey his parent? The belief concerning the extent of one's freedom clearly appears "in a variety of situations,"[80] and this belief can be frustrated either because the individual is prevented from attaining a desirable goal or is required to behave in a particular manner, or because—paradoxically—the freedom to select alternatives can lead to uncertainty and perplexity.[81]

The individual may deny that he has the freedom to act by disclaiming responsibility and shifting that responsibility to someone else. The originator of the same experiments in which most normal college students and other adult Americans were willing to administer what they believed to be severe shocks because the experimenter in a white coat told them to do so in the interest of science has tried to point to the implications of his investigations:

... ordinary people, simply doing their jobs, and without any particular hostility on their part, can become agents in a terrible destructive process. Moreover, even when the destructive effects of their work become patently clear, and they are asked to carry out actions incompatible with fundamental standards of morality, relatively few people have the resources needed to resist authority. A variety of inhibitions against disobeying authority come into play and successfully keep the person in his place.[82]

The best-known instance of this process is that of Adolf Eichmann, the SS officer who was tried by an Israeli court for the murder of thousands of Jews and Gentiles. Apparently he felt no guilt because, he said, exterminating such persons was part of the plan of the Nazi state to which he belonged. He was only obeying orders of superior officers. The judges at the trial considered him responsible, and he was executed. Eichmann's plea was echoed by many other Nazis: "*Ja, was konnte ich denn, war ja nur ein kleiner Mann?*" ("What could I do, I was only a little man?")[83] This view of oneself has been called "the banality of evil,"[84] but why banal? Only if we assume, as the experimenter quoted above suggests, that most of us under the circumstances potentially are Evildoers like Eichmann.

In another context, a social scientist has contended: "In order to persuade a good and moral man to *do* evil, then, it is not necessary first to persuade him to *become* evil. It is only necessary to teach him that he is doing good. No one . . . thinks of himself as a son of a bitch."[85] But, it may be contended, not everyone is a potential Eichmann, not everyone allows his own or society's norms to be transformed, not everyone can be persuaded to become an Evildoer. For, as already indicated in connection with the discussion of motives, only men with certain predispositions commit evil deeds.[86] Those who became SS men (of course, with exceptions) and especially those who participated with some satisfaction in the activities of the concentration camps (perhaps with fewer exceptions) possessed personalities or traits inclining them toward such activities. Save for one man, none of the eight "SS killers," according to the psychiatrist who examined them, "would have been likely to become 'common murderers' in normal conditions"; rather "their instigatory triggering was not a sudden, solitary experience, but a process extending over time, shared with teammates in a facilitating group setting."[87] Even though their freedom and their sense of responsibility were thus curtailed as a result of a series of events and the situation itself, they might or could have participated with less enthusiasm and with more misgiving. Again in the experiments involving ostensible electric shocks, there were some American subjects who refused to cooperate or who stopped shocking the ostensible Victim before the shock appeared to be too severe; and these persons had a "higher" concept of morality as measured on a standardized paper-and-pencil scale.[88] Perhaps the subjects could exercise their higher morality more easily than the SS men could because the confederate being ostensibly shocked seemed attractive, whereas the Victims in the Nazi camps had been previously vilified and dehumanized. In addition, those with certain personality traits—notably a higher degree of dogmatism and approval seeking and a low degree of self-esteem—*may* be more likely to administer severe shocks in this situation than those with traits inclining them in the opposite direction, although the intimacy of the relation between the Evildoer and the Victim may be more important.[89]

It should be apparent that evildoing is seldom a kind of activity in which Evildoers easily and joyfully engage *when*—and the conjunction is important—they realize, consciously or unconsciously, the stigma others or they themselves attach to what they contemplate or what they have done. They need to fortify themselves with all kinds of beliefs and to perceive the potential and actual Victims in a particular way. After they have harmed another human being, they *may* feel the need to justify what they have done, to try to compensate the victim, or even to punish themselves.[90] Their inhibitions, their guilt, call it what you will, does not mean that evil can easily be prevented or combated because both they themselves and their society are teeming with compelling ways to circumvent what their better selves would avoid.

NOTES

1. Ludwig von Mises, *Theory and History* (New Haven: Yale University Press, 1957), p. 90.

2. Felix Gilbert, "European and American Historiography," in John Higham, ed., *History* (Englewood Cliffs: Prentice-Hall, 1965), pp. 315-87.

3. R. L. Franklin, *Freewill and Determinism* (New York: Humanities Press, 1968), p. 2.

4. Nevill Sanford and Craig Comstock, "Epilogue," in Nevill Sanford et al., eds., *Sanctions for Evil* (San Francisco: Jossey-Bass, 1971), pp. 323-36.

5. Richard Cavendish, *The Powers of Evil* (New York: Putnam's, 1975), p. 25.

6. C. E. M. Joad, *The Recovery of Belief* (London: Faber and Faber, 1952), p. 23, italics his.

7. C. E. M. Joad, *Guide to Modern Wickedness* (London: Faber and Faber, 1939), p. 31.

8. Ibid., p. 55.

9. David Bidney, "The Varieties of Human Freedom," in David Bidney, ed., *The Concept of Freedom in Anthropology* (Hague: Mouton, 1963), pp. 11-34.

10. Cf. Henry V. Dicks, *Licensed Mass Murder* (New York: Basic Books, 1972), p. 90.

11. Ayn Rand, *The Virtue of Selfishness* (New York: New American Library, 1964), pp. 46, 50.

12. Edward Glover, *War, Sadism, and Pacifism* (London: Allen & Unwin, 1933), p. 186.

13. Stanley Milgram, "The Compulsion to Do Evil," *Patterns of Prejudice* 1, no. 6 (1967): 3-7.

14. Karl E. Scheibe, "Legitimized Aggression and the Assignment of Evil," 1933), p. 186.

15. Bernard L. Diamond, "Failures of Identification and Sociopathic Behavior," in Sanford et al., *Sanctions for Evil*, pp. 125-35.

16. David R. Walters, *Physical and Sexual Abuse of Children* (Bloomington: Indiana University Press, 1975), p. 4.

17. Philip P. Hallie, *The Paradox of Cruelty* (Middletown: Wesleyan University Press, 1969), p. 29.

18. Erich Fromm, *The Heart of Man* (New York: Harper & Row, 1964), p. 131.

19. Martin L. Hoffman, "Conscience, Personality, and Socialization Techniques," *Human Development* 13 (1970): 90-126.

20. Daniel R. Miller and Guy E. Swanson, *Inner Conflict and Defense* (New York: Holt, 1960), p. 26.

21. Cited by Scheibe, "Legitimized Aggression."

22. Yahya Armajani, *Iran* (Englewood Cliffs: Prentice-Hall, 1972), p. 20.

23. Reinhold Niebuhr, *The Nature and Destiny of Man* (New York: Scribner's, 1949), 1: 167-68.

24. Ibid., p. 96.

25. Ernest Becker, *The Structure of Evil* (New York: George Braziller, 1968), p. 195.

26. Roy R. Grinker and John P. Spiegel, *Men under Stress* (Philadelphia: Blakiston, 1945), pp. 38-41.

27. Avery Craven, *The Repressible Conflict, 1830-1861* (University: Louisiana State University Press, 1939), pp. 27, 64.

28. Sandra J. Ball-Rokeach, "Values and Violence," *American Sociological Review* 38 (1973): 736-49.

29. Hannah Arendt, *Eichmann in Jerusalem* (New York: Viking, 1964), p. 277.

30. Ezra Pound, *Confucius* (New York: New Directions, 1969), p. 199.

31. Dicks, *Licensed Mass Murder*, pp. 70-71.

32. Ibid., p. 124.

33. Julian B. Rotter, "Generalized Expectancies for Internal versus External Control of Reinforcement," *Psychological Monographs* 80, no. 609 (1960).

34. Herbert M. Lefcourt, "Recent Developments in the Study of Locus of Control," in Brendan A. Maher, ed., *Progress in Experimental Personality Research* (New York: Academic Press, 1972), 6: 1-39. Other summaries include: Paul D. Hersch and Karl E. Scheibe, "Reliability and Validity of Internal-External Control as a Personality Dimension," *Journal of Consulting Psychology* 31 (1967): 609-13; Herbert L. Mirels, "Dimensions of Internal versus External Control," *Journal of Consulting and Clinical Psychology* 34 (1970): 226-28; Julian B. Rotter and Ray C. Mulay, "Internal versus External Control of Reinforcement and Decision Time," *Journal of Personality and Social Psychology* 2 (1965): 598-604; and Steven J. Sherman, "Internal-External Control and Its Relationship to Attitude Change under Different Social Influence Techniques," *Journal of Personality and Social Psychology* 26 (1973): 23-29.

35. Dorothy J. Hochreich, "Defensive Externality and Attribution of Responsibility," *Journal of Personality* 42 (1974): 543-57.

36. Herbert M. Lefcourt, "The Function of the Illusions of Control and Freedom," *American Psychologist* 28 (1973): 417-25.

37. Esther Battle and Julia B. Rotter, "Children's Feelings and Personal Control as Related to Social Class and Ethnic Group," *Journal of Personality* 31 (1963): 482-90.

38. Richard Ryckman and Martin F. Sherman, "Locus of Control and Student Reaction to the Watergate Break-in," *Journal of Social Psychology* 99 (1976): 305-06.

39. Donald Granberg and William May, "I-E and Orientations toward the Vietnam War," *Journal of Social Psychology* 88 (1972): 157-58. See also Barney Rosen and Robin Salling, "Political Participation as a Function of Internal-External Locus of Control," *Psychological Reports* 29 (1971): 880-82.

40. Dorothy Hochreich, "Internal-External Control and Reaction to the My Lai Courts-Martial," *Journal of Applied Social Psychology* 2 (1972): 319-25. See also Susan P. Sanger and Henry A. Alker, "Dimensions of Internal-External Locus of Control and the Women's Liberation Movement, *Journal of Social Issues* 28 (1972): 115-29.

41. Alexander Tolor and Richard F. LeBlanc, "Personality Correlates of Alienation," *Journal of Consulting and Clinical Psychology* 37 (1971): 444.

42. H. A. Witkin et al., *Psychological Differentiation* (New York: Wiley, 1962), pp. 155, 366-67.

43. P. S. Fry, "Children's Social Sensitivity, Altruism, and Self-Gratification," *Journal of Social Psychology* 98 (1976): 77-88.

44. Norman Frohlich, "Self-Interest or Altruism, What Difference?" *Journal of Conflict Resolution* 18 (1974): 55-73.

45. Alfred H. Bloom, "Two Dimensions of Moral Reasoning," *Journal of Social Psychology* 101 (1977): 29-44. See also Hugh Gash, "Moral Development," *Genetic Psychology Monographs* 93 (1976): 91-111.

46. Shalom H. Schwartz, "Moral Decision Making and Behavior," in J. Macaulay and L. Berkowitz, eds., *Altruism and Helping Behavior* (New York: Academic Press, 1970), pp. 127-41.

47. Ernest Becker, *Escape from Evil* (New York: Free Press, 1975), p. xvii.

48. Cf. Kurt H. Wolff, "For a Sociology of Evil," *Journal of Social Issues* 25, no. 1 (1969): 111-25.

49. Vivian Charles Walsh, *Scarcity and Evil* (Englewood Cliffs: Prentice-Hall, 1961), p. 81.

50. Seymour Feshbach, William B. Stiles, and Edward Bitter, "The Reinforcing Effect of Witnessing Aggression," *Journal of Experimental Research in Personality* 2 (1967): 133-39.

51. Rollo May, *Power and Innocence* (New York: Norton, 1972), pp. 23-27.

52. Alfred Adler, cited by Becker, *Structure of Evil*, p. 52.

53. Hallie, *Paradox of Cruelty*, p. 17.

54. May, *Power and Innocence*, p. 166.

55. Philip G. Zimbardo, "The Human Choice," in William J. Arnold and David Levine, eds., *Nebraska Symposium on Motivation, 1969* (Lincoln: University of Nebraska Press, 1969), pp. 237-307.

56. Glover, *War*, p. 69.

57. J. K. Zawodny, *Death in the Forest* (Notre Dame: University of Notre Dame Press, 1962).

58. All the quotations and the data come from Robert B. Textor, *A Cross-Cultural Summary* (New Haven: HRAF Press, 1967), category 420.

59. Robert M. Liebert, John M. Neale, and Emily S. Davidson, *The Early Window* (New York: Pergamon, 1973).

60. Ronald E. Smith, Lisa Smythe, and Douglas Lien, "Inhibition of Helping Behavior by a Similar or Dissimilar Nonreactive Fellow Bystander," *Journal of Personality and Social Psychology* 23 (1972): 414-19.

61. Irving L. Janis, *Victims of Groupthink* (Boston: Houghton Mifflin, 1972).

62. David Irving, *The Destruction of Dresden* (London: William Kimber, 1963), pp. 3-30.

63. Lewis M. Killian, "The Significance of Multiple-Group Membership in Disaster," *American Journal of Sociology* (1952): 309-17.

64. Lewis Merkin, Jr., *They Chose Honor* (New York: Harper & Row, 1974), pp. 19-32.

65. Dicks, *Licensed Mass Murder*, pp. 55-56.

66. Neil J. Smelser, "Some Determinants of Destructive Behavior," in Sanford et al., *Sanctions for Evil*, pp. 15-24.

67. May Edel and Abraham Edel, *Anthropology and Ethics* (Cleveland: Case Western Reserve University Press, 1968), p. 88.

68. Scheibe, "Legitimized Aggression."

69. Ellen Berscheid and Elaine Hatfield Walster, *Interpersonal Attraction* (Reading: Addison-Wesley, 1969), pp. 15, 14-20.

70. Terrence Des Pres, *The Survivor* (New York: Oxford University Press, 1976), pp. 54-61.

71. Dicks, *Licensed Mass Murder*, 89-90.

72. Erich Fromm, *The Anatomy of Human Destructiveness* (New York: Holt, Rinehart and Winston, 1973), p. 122.

73. Zimbardo, "Human Choice," pp. 251, 296.

74. Edward Diener et al., "Effects of Altered Responsibility, Cognitive Set, and Modeling on Physical Aggression and Deindividuation," *Journal of Personality and Social Psychology* 31 (1975): 328-37.

75. Zimbardo, "Human Choice," pp. 263-71.

76. Robert I. Watson, Jr., "Investigation into Deindividuation Using a Cross-cultural Survey Technique," *Journal of Personality and Social Psychology* 25 (1973): 342-45.

77. Gerald D. Robin, "The Executioner," *British Journal of Sociology* 15 (1964): 234-53.

78. Everett C. Hughes, "Good People and Dirty Work," *Social Problems* 10 (1962): 3-11.

79. Audrey I. Richards, "Freedom, Communications, and Transport," in Bidney, ed., *Concept of Freedom*, pp. 49-60.

80. Ivan D. Steiner, "Perceived Freedom," in Leonard Berkowitz, ed., *Advances in Experimental Social Psychology, 1970* (New York: Academic Press, 1970), pp. 187-248.

81. Cf. Eric Fromm, *Escape from Freedom* (New York: Holt, Rinehart & Winston, 1941).

82. Stanley Milgram, *Obedience to Authority* (New York: Harper & Row, 1974), p. 6.

83. Dicks, *Licensed Mass Murders*, p. 37.

84. Arendt, *Eichmann*, p. 252.

85. William Ryan, *Blaming the Victim* (New York: Pantheon, 1971), p. 19.

86. Schwartz, "Moral Decision Making," pp. 128-30.

87. Dicks, *Licensed Mass Murder*, p. 273.

88. Florence R. Miale and Michael Selzer, *The Nuremberg Mind* (New York: Quadrangle, 1975), pp. 12-13.

89. Lefcourt, "Function of the Illusions."

90. Berscheid and Walster, *Interpersonal Attraction*, p. 21.

8

PREVENTION: EVILDOERS

Two fuzzy lines of demarcation now make their appearance. The first separates the prevention from the combating of evildoing. Certainly evil is combated when it is prevented, and it is prevented from recurring when it is combated or when therapy is administered. But the emphasis is somewhat different if one seeks to prevent a brushfire from occurring or to stamp one out after the blaze has begun. The other line is between Evildoers and Victims. In both instances attention is directed separately upon prevention and combating. Again the emphasis varies: a society or an individual would prevent or combat Evildoers or evildoing in order to avoid the suffering of Victims, but individuals would prevent themselves from becoming Victims or would combat evil after they have become Victims.

Whatever or wherever the lines are, no panacea will be unveiled in this analysis or anywhere. Both the past and the present teem with what have turned out or doubtless will turn out to be delusions either in whole or in part. "The Renaissance," a socially minded theologian concludes, "was wrong in imagining that the possibilities of good would gradually eliminate the possibilities of evil," inasmuch as "a false ideal of progress was implicit in the curious compound of Christian eschatology and classical rationalism which was the foundation of Renaissance spirituality."[1] Quite similarly during the late nineteenth and early twentieth centuries, it was believed that the world was really making what was then called progress, and hence that evil was gradually being eradicated, to be replaced by a better future.[2] We know now that such progress was a vague goal, achieved in some fields—the conquering of many diseases and the consequent increase in life expectancy, the tremendous advances in knowledge especially in the sciences, perhaps the alleviation of aspects of poverty (though with an increase in slums and often a deterioration of working conditions in factories and mines)—but certainly not in other fields such as aesthetics, philosophy, the standard of living in developing countries, and the curbing of war. The optimism provided by the notion of progress, a historian suggests, may have been misleading; it caused us all to underestimate the inertia within society and hence the resistance to change. Many countries outside the Western orbit have now also acquired the same faith in a progressive future, or at least their leaders have; and so, like us a century ago, most of them are motivated to introduce technological and political changes, however ill founded their faith may turn out to be.[3] Actually, most thoughtful persons in the West—and perhaps the more realistic ones elsewhere—realize that we do not know how to combat the evils that hurt and corrupt.

A discussion concerning the various panaceas would be endless. It would involve an evaluation of all the reforms ever proposed. In practice, short of a real revolution, what happens is that we chip away at segments of one or more problems. Any clergyman, educator, psychiatrist, or parent gropes toward a solution. Schools and moral tracts have not succeeded in ridding our times of evil. Have they diminished it?

Another argument against having overflowing faith in panaceas suggests that evildoing includes so many different actions that no single solution can ever be universally valid. One summary of the experimental literature prior to the 1970s—a literature which suffers from the usual limitations—suggests that antisocial actions such as "aggression, cheating, and exploitation have been shown to be influenced by the behavior of models, proximity of the victim and of authority, judgment of ethical risk, and Level of Moral Thought."[4] Such factors have obvious counterparts among those discussed in the last chapter in connection with the genesis of Evildoers, but here we can see that even in very artificial laboratory situations there is multicausality—and where there is multicausality, there is not likely to be a single cure.

Recognizing evil is by itself no panacea. Recognition is a purely intellectual act, which may or may not lead to action. It seems too easy to say, as Socrates did, that "if a man knows the good, then he cannot choose evil" and hence that evil results from ignorance.[5] Some crimes are intentionally committed in the full knowledge that they are crimes, although "full knowledge" is a slippery term not easily pinned down psychologically. We may hope that the rational, Theologic Man will always select the good and not the evil course of action, and we may argue morally and legally that he should; but we know he is driven by forces other than rationality. He is as much a hope and myth as Economic Man. And yet recognition, however imperfect or irrational Theologic Man is, may be a first step toward preventing or combating evil.

Recognition may provide the motivation to think and to act. The idea can remain a dream inside the Judge, it can become the subject of conversation among his friends (and thus he exhibits his originality or brilliance), it can be pushed into prominence by being communicated to persons with power, and so on. Does the Judge with an idea have an obligation to see it realized? Here is a Pandora's box of possibilities ranging from the view that each Judge has only a single life to live (and so self-sacrifice is not always a summum bonum but may contain a touch of egotism) to the conviction that allowing good ideas to atrophy for good or bad reasons may be a supreme evil. The critical challenge is to determine and then create the circumstances that may induce anyone to take action against a person who is about to or has become an Evildoer. In most abstract terms the challenge can be met by saying, very simply, that the motivation can be as diverse as that behind any imaginable action and that the goal must be that of creating situations and sanctions likely to inhibit the appearance of evil proneness. The situations and sanctions can be intuited in concrete form as we survey the ways to prevent that proneness and to combat evildoing.

On a theoretical level, the problem of preventing evil can be phrased in manageable form: produce persons who cannot or will not commit evil. Breed them the way plants and animals within limits can be bred. But can this be done with human beings? And here there must be a burst of optimism: the breeding involves not eugenics but changing the conditions in the society that give rise to Evildoers. If one of the most significant roots of evil is aggression—at least a special kind of aggression, malignant or destructive aggression—that is not genetically determined but acquired under special conditions in the milieu, then we ought to be able to create evil-free persons by changing the environment as well as our socialization and educational methods.[6] Utopian?

Of course, but the dream comes as close to reality as experience and knowledge permit.

Evil is not likely to occur in an environment that does not tempt individuals to commit evil deeds and that satisfies their basic and acquired needs. An influential, confident behaviorist declares, "We change the relative strengths of responses by differential reinforcement of alternative courses of action; we do not change something called a preference."[7] In an easier sentence: good behavior can be encouraged by the milieu. Yes, yes, yes; but someone has to produce the milieu that encourages the good behavior and that someone, if the same recommendation is followed, must in turn be motivated to make the changes, presumably by other reinforcing agents in his milieu. An infinite regress appears that punctures the purity of the behavioristic position, a puncture that can be repaired only by maintaining that the individuals changing the milieu are themselves responding to a special portion of that milieu. Here we bump our heads into some kind of deterministic doctrine (cultural, economic, historical) and a stress upon leadership. There is no escape from the regress since the "differential reinforcement" must be engineered by someone who thus leads the way. That leader somehow must be induced to have "a preference" for one type of reinforcement rather than another. It is a bit glib, therefore, for the same behaviorist to assert that "the man that man has made is the product of the culture man has devised," for clearly the referents of the three men are different in each instance.[8] Also it is necessary to remind ourselves that a reinforcing agent is effective only when the human being possesses a residue from previous experience that enables him to respond, and that residue might well be called a preference.

Facilitating the right kind of persons must mean in large part preventing the kinds of frustration leading to aggressive acts, which in themselves are evil. Since "a frustration is an event that often increases hopelessness," it follows that a frustrated person cannot be a Theologic Man because he is not likely to be capable of making a wise decision or, in metaphysical terms, his free will will be blocked.[9] Frustrations of various kinds may be inevitable, but they can be reduced—let us hope, however vainly. A just political order in which individuals feel secure (vague though that concept is) and in which they have their basic and sensitive needs satisfied is the prescription one can more easily state than achieve. Both the reactionary and the radical movements of our time have striven to attain such a utopia, sometimes with passing success but never everlastingly. To the extent that frustrations remain, evil must always be ubiquitous and can never be completely eradicated, although its scope and frequency can be limited. Again there is no panacea, but we know that physical well-being, adequate income, old-age benefits, security, recreational facilities, love, and so forth are not clichés but take on deep meaning in programs or behavior. They are, in brief, the prerequisites for creating the conditions in which Theologic Man might conceivably have the opportunity to function.

Any kind of situation in which aggression may be generated or aggravated is usually to be avoided. The whole sphere of interpersonal relations becomes relevant to the problem of evil. Every condition that *may* increase aggressive impulses—such as the excessive (maybe even the moderate) consumption of alcohol—ought to be avoided, but the conditions are both numerous and uncontrollable.[10] In virtually every society for which evidence exists, consuming alcoholic beverages has "beneficial" effects too.

On a psychological level it is difficult or impossible to prevent evil when certain beliefs exist within the social heritage and are then perpetuated by leaders, the mass media, and the educational system.[11] There is a long string of beliefs associated with war, which can facilitate that evil: my country, right or wrong: every citizen must obey: we have a manifest destiny; Lebensraum is needed; all's fair in love and war; those people hate us; this must be done in the line of duty. Can anyone develop impulses that resist such categorical imperatives? Calm skepticism seems justified.

In theory the existence of sanctions within the society ought to prevent evil, for then the person anticipates that punishment is probable or certain: the plan may not succeed; somehow the police will apprehend him. "Perhaps the most general and most important influence on aggression," one summary of the experimental literature suggests, *may* be "the probability of reward or punishment for aggressive behavior."[12] Investigations have been conducted to determine, for example, which of the following procedures more effectively promotes learning: intermittent or certain punishment or reward; punishment or reward; punishment that is anticipated or administered after the forbidden act. And the results? With many *perhapses* and *mays* thrown in, especially since much of experimental work has been inspired by animal research, the first of the pairs in the above trios *may* have some advantages.[13]

Orthodox Christianity seems to adhere to the last of these findings by providing a devastating threat both to thought and action: "God has foreknowledge of all that happens,"[14] and hence any kind of evil, though undetected by one's peers, may lead to everlasting damnation. To our immense sorrow, however, we are aware that momentary passions or reckless splurges can overcome dreaded anticipations. People commit crimes even when they know capital punishment can be the penalty; in the United States, for example, "most murders are not premeditated, but rather are impulsive crimes of passion often committed under the influence of alcohol when guns happen to be handy."[15] And we know that the crime rate continued to be high in England up to the eighteenth century, even though the punishments were gruesome and the number of offenses punishable by death increased (for example, death was the penalty for being armed or disguised in a park containing deer).[16] The figures on recidivism in modern society indicate unquestionably that punishment does not prevent convicted Evildoers from committing crimes in the future. Compliance with society's sanctions is never complete; the attractions of evildoing from any standpoint are overwhelmingly great for some persons under particular circumstances.

A danger in any kind of punishment, especially that imposed by law, is that only those who are apprehended and convicted suffer and not those in the society who directly or indirectly may be responsible either for the conditions producing the evildoer or for failing to establish the kinds of sanctions that might prevent the evildoing.[17] It is too easy, in other words, to locate scapegoats. The riskiest, the most challenging action against an evildoer is capital punishment; beheading, hanging, shooting, and electrocuting are external acts that cannot be retrieved and that gives human beings the power ordinarily allocated only to fate, spirits, deities, disease, and old age.[18]

Punishment, therefore, is not necessarily an effective way to prevent evil. And yet we cannot turn the argument upside down and abolish punishment for evildoing[19] because then presumably whatever deterrent influence punishment has would be removed, and evildoing would run no risks at all. We also know or intuit that the presence of an authority such as a policeman or a parent does prevent evildoing, in the short run at the very least. At the same time we must heed a statement made at the beginning of the last century: "I call upon you to remember that cruel punishments have an inevitable tendency to produce cruelty in people."[20]

As we grope to resolve the problem, we might possibly find hints from an examination of how non-Western societies have dealt with the punishment of evil. Among the Luo in East Africa, violence is considered to be "an unnecessary loss of control, or at best a calculated necessary last resort to secure goals which have been carefully weighed and assessed as to the possible supernatural and social consequences." Violence thus is taboo except under unusual circumstances, and even then its possible supernatural consequences demand "physical and spiritual cleansing of the most exacting nature."[21] Thus when the taboo breaker kills an enemy, he must shave his own head three days after returning from battle; he may not enter his own village until a live fowl is hung around his neck, after which the fowl is decapitated and its head left hanging from his neck; a feast is given in honor of the Victim, so that his spirit will not return to trouble the victor.[22] We are not told how effective this method is, but at least we glimpse the technique: a combination of punishment, through symbols and isolation, and of reward by being restored to the society. On a theoretical level it has been persuasively argued that the most one learns from punishment is only how to avoid the punishment in the future and not how to behave in that future.[23] In fact, in Polynesia where the word *taboo* originated, there is an equally clear concept, *noa*, meaning the contrary of taboo. The taboo breaker, in short, may find salvation but not easily.

Among the same Luo another established taboo does not effectively inhibit the designated person from breaking it. Women with a strong liking for forbidden foods are said to eat them anyhow in spite of threatened punishment; thus a pregnant woman does not avoid drinking hot gruel even though she has been told it will scald the baby.[24] Perhaps the difference between the two taboos can be traced to the nature of the sanctions: the supernatural punishment following violence can really make the individual anxious, whereas the eating of forbidden foods may have no immediately perceivable consequences.

Whether punishment in fact prevents evil, every society punishes Evildoers or threatens to do so either through its own or supernatural means. Those who are not Evildoers are likely to believe that Evildoers either suffer here and now or will suffer in the future. Whether they in fact do is an unsettled empirical question. If the source of their punishment comes from outside themselves, there may be a basis in reality for inferring their misery. A Judge may make a wild inferential leap and assume that they are punishing themselves: their consciences really bother them. He thus derives satisfaction from his own state of innocence.

"Beliefs about evil supernatural agencies, thought to menace and prey on human beings, are known in all primitive societies," it has been declared as the first sentence in a book about "the powers of evil."[25] Whether or not the assertion is literally true—anthropologists can usually find an exception to any generalization somewhere—is unimportant, for at least we know that the belief in such agencies as sources of punishment for taboo breaking is widespread. Buddhism provides its adherents with "a complete system of future rewards and punishments."[26] The ancient Egyptians believed that sin would produce misfortune or premature death here and now and would be punished after death.[27] The old Teutonic tribes, especially those in the north, subscribed to "the concept of a coming retribution in another world."[28]

Both to prevent and combat evil, in the abstract or concrete, evil itself is usually personified in some intelligible form. Whatever is personified as evil must be avoided, for it has power to do harm and thus creates Evildoers, who are also Victims. The forms vary and include spirits, witches, and ordinary human beings whose evil eyes, intentions, or actions lead to evil. It seems legitimate to speculate again concerning the possibility that often these so-called agents of evil function, consciously or unconsciously, as scapegoats for the Evildoer who thus would avoid punishment by disclaiming responsibility. In Christianity, one fallen angel in particular—first it was thought and taught that he was cast out of heaven because he was jealous of God, then because he suffered from pride—is considered to be the real or metaphorical source of all or most evil, and hence it is he who must be avoided and combated: the Devil or Satan (who is the Adversary).[29] A loving god cannot be held responsible—and it must be recalled that the gods of ancient Greece were both good and bad and that Jehovah was a stern deity who on occasion brought destruction upon mankind or particular individuals.

The Devil is so important in Christian thought that he has his own story or history. He has evolved as men have changed, and notions about him have undergone a radical revision. In modern times it has been contended by a prelate of the Catholic church that "For a Catholic, Satan is *Someone.* Satan is not an abstraction, an invention, a character in fiction, the hero of a novel. Neither is Satan the mythical explanation provided by ignorance for those nervous disorders which are properly the domain of medicine, and have nothing to do with theology."[30]

It is asserted that "the presence of Satan in our age and time" is likely or certain because of the existence of nazism and of "communism in immense countries such as Russia and the People's Republic of China."[31] Evidence that an individual human being has become possessed by the Devil includes "use or understanding of an unknown tongue; knowledge of distant or hidden facts; and exhibitions of physical powers exceeding the age or condition of the subject," as well as "other phenomena of the same sort."[32] Baudelaire's warning is quoted with approval: "The Evil's deepest wile is to persuade us that he does not exist." "No one wants to believe in evil, really, above all, not in an evil spirit" since "to admit the existence of evil means a responsibility, and no one wants that responsibility"; consequently, "that is the opening through which Tortoise [the Devil] crawls, stilling all suspicion, making everything seem normal and natural."[33] Under these circumstances, it is "only to priests whose high moral worth protects them from all danger, and whose knowledge and judgment enable them to make a sure estimate of the case put before them, that the Church entrusts the dangerous task of pitting themselves against the devil."[34] The alleged increase in exorcisms in the present day must represent the growing belief that evil deeds are becoming more numerous, as well as the consequent conviction that divine assistance is needed.[35]

The conditions under which evil is attributed to occult rather than mundane powers are difficult to specify. I guess that the appearance in the dreams of complicated symbols that are difficult or impossible to decode plays some role.[36] The Devil is a versatile creature who can be presented in many terrifying forms. The sacred book of Buddhism describes how he appeared as he attacked the redeemer Bodhisattva:

The devil . . . prepared his mighty army, four legion strong and valiant in combat, a fearful army that struck terror into the hearts of all who beheld it, an army such as had never been seen or heard of before, by men or gods. This army had the power to take on all manner of different appearances, transforming itself endlessly in a hundred million ways. Its body and hands and feet were wrapped in the coils of a hundred thousand serpents, and in its hands were swords, bows, arrows, pikes, axes, mallets, rockets, pestles, sticks, chains, clubs, discuses, and all other instruments of war. Its body was protected by excellent breast plates. Its heads and hands and feet turned in all directions. Its eyes and faces were flaming; its stomachs, feet, and hands of all shapes. Its faces glittered in terrible splendor; its faces and teeth were of all shapes, its dog teeth enormous, fearful to behold. Its tongues were as rough as mats of hair, its eyes red and glittering, like those of the black serpent full of venom. Some were spitting the venom of serpents, and some, having taken the venom in their hands, were eating it. Some, like the Garudas, having drawn out of the sea human flesh and blood, feet, hands, heads, livers, entrails, and bones, were eating them. Some had bodies of flame, livid, black, bluish, red, yellow; some had misshapen eyes, as hollow as empty wells, inflamed, gouged or squinting; some had eyes that were contorted, glittering, out of shape; some were carrying burning mountains, approaching majestically, mounted on other burning mountains. Some, having torn up trees by their roots, were rushing toward the Bodhisattva. Some had the ears of stags, pigs, elephants—hanging ears or boars' ears. Some had no ears at all. Some, with stomachs like mountains and withered bodies made from a mass of skeleton bones, had broken noses; others had stomachs like rounded jars, feet like the feet of cranes, with skin and flesh and blood all dried up, and their ears and noses, their hands and feet, their eyes and heads all lopped off. . . .

Some with the skin of oxen, asses, boars, ichneumons, stags, rams, beetles, cats, apes, wolves, and jackals, were spitting snake venom, and—swallowing balls of fire, breathing flame, sending down a rain of brass and molten iron, calling up black clouds, bringing black night, and making a great noise—were running toward the Bodhisattva. . . .[37]

Burning everlastingly in hell is a prospect supposedly counteracting whatever advantages accrue from evildoing. Less direct but just as anxiety producing are other threats: ancestors may intervene; justice in some vague but retributive form hovers over the Evildoer. His guilt may pervade his dreams, traces of which turn into nightmares or haunt his waking hours.

The nature of the taboos and of the real or threatened punishments for breaking them is learned gradually during infancy and childhood; breeding persons who will not become Evildoers, consequently, depends in large part on the kind of socialization encouraged or demanded by the society. It is clear that one of the most efficient ways to learn any kind of behavior, including the avoidance of evil, is to follow a good model, whether it be a person (such as a friend or parent) or a hypothetical one (such as a particular god or prophet). One adopts his advice; one imitates his behavior; one identifies with him so strongly that details are unimportant; one becomes (or at least feels) like him. To some extent the socializers in any society—parents, educators, clergymen—serve this function, and hence obedience to them is usually considered a cardinal virtue not only to secure that obedience as such but also to rear a human being on the side of the angels. Any society, however, provides many evil models with prestige and influence. There is likely to be a braggard or antihero who appears to and affects the young. One need only mention the sleezy slime of most television programs in the West (which, alas, are exported to countries who cannot afford their own programs) to suggest the forces of evil arrayed against what some, maybe most, Judges would consider good models. The ability of the child to comprehend the example of a model *may* be related to his moral development and that in turn perhaps to the skill with which he is able to role play the behavior of his own peers.[38]

Which traits should be encouraged and discouraged during socialization if non-Evildoers are to be produced? The clue here must come from the previous chapter in which an effort was made to locate the traits leading away from and toward evildoing. Self-mastery, patience, and internal locus of control, relative independence of conditions in the immediate environment, sensitivity regarding others, altruism, humanism: these are the traits that seem to incline individuals to avoid evildoing. Others could be added, such as confidence in one's own identity or a sense of responsibility.[39] If only the following conclusion, based on two paper-and-pencil tests and one behavioral measure given to a sample of American women undergraduates, could have universal validity: "These findings strongly suggest that felt responsibility for outcome together with competence at analytic functioning mediate principled morality."[40] Even so, with such a guide to socialization, we would still be left with the problem of how best to achieve individuals with those proclivities. In addition, the traits themselves may not be controllable or, if controllable, unrelated to evildoing. The locus-of-control trait, for example, *may* be associated with the fortuitous fact of birth order, though only in the case of males in our society;[41] and its association with evil-related attitudes *may* be very slight or close to zero.

Conceivably there are attitudes toward other persons that can be taught and that may inhibit evil proneness. Here we must leap into the unprovable and try to absorb the experience of mankind. First of all, respect for the integrity of the other person seems to be a virtue associated with good and not evil. A Judge may consider lying a mild or severe form of evil and may be convinced that lying under most circumstances should be curbed and punished. His judgment might be different, however, if he discovers the reasons for the lie. This is not to suggest that comprehension means forgiveness, only that it may indicate the therapy to be employed, the means to combat the evil; forgiveness is another matter. The petty thief who mugs a Victim is not respecting him. It is admittedly much easier to designate another person as a member of some other group—he is a Frenchman, a Muslim, a South African—and thus to make inferences concerning him from real or imagined knowledge about that group than to judge him as a unique person. His individuality is not properly valued. Even though all of us may be solipsistically encased, we can try to communicate and to comprehend the other person; when we succeed, even partially, the chances of committing evil may diminish.[42] Again and again, in an enduring document such as the Bible, one finds an admonition suggesting by indirection the value of forthrightness: "But let your communication be, Yea, yea; Nay, nay: for whatsoever is more than these cometh of evil."[43] In different words, do not equivocate; give a plain *yes* or *no* answer to the other person and in that manner demonstrate your trust.

A more powerful hymn may be sung in favor of the cultivation of love, all kinds of love ranging from compassion and friendship to eros and amor.[44] Whether this magic circle can be extended to include, at least in the abstract, the abolition of hate and war through loving mankind is a problem puzzling all the great religions striving to accomplish that feat. Let us, however, not grow sloppily sentimental about love, integrity, or the comprehension of other persons. Each of us, even if we live in the bustle of an extended, gregarious family, at some point requires privacy. A sensitive anthropologist has issued the challenge:

. . . I myself do not want to be understood. I want to be known, to be recognized, to generate joy or outrage or disgust; but I don't want to be understood. If I am, my very integrity is molested; it is disintegrated, probed, analyzed—all with the very best motives. The minute a person understands me, encounter is blocked, befogged by the theory that must underlie his diagnosis. Beyond that, I find in understanding something of condescension that is often a dimension of kindly attempts in our society.[45]

Yes, we live with our fellow men in a social world, but we would also respect and treasure our own feelings, fantasies, and integrity.

Certainly during socialization the individual is and must be taught the principles of morality to be followed. Each person, we know, has stored within him sentences enabling him to reason and guide his behavior. These sentences are likely to be codified within the society in the form of proverbs and commandments. Everyone—or almost everyone—knows them; not everyone follows them. Principles of this sort, to be effective, must first of all be understood and then must dominate man's existence. That neither assumption may be true is tacitly admitted by every clergyman who has ever preached a sermon: he explains the biblical injunctions to the congregation (or at least gives his own interpretation), and then he tries to have them comprehend how they can be applied to everyday existence.

Actually, however, in a complex society it is by no means certain which ethical principles should be taught. Two kinds of ethics, for example, have been ascribed, on the basis of paper-and-pencil evidence, to American undergraduates: one is called that of responsibility, for it stresses the value of law and social institutions and questions the natural benevolence of human beings; the other is that of moral intuitionism, for it ascribes evil to institutions and believes in the natural goodness of human beings.[46] Which system of ethics should be emphasized? The question cannot be answered empirically by trying to determine whether men are "naturally" good or bad; whether one weltanschauung can be learned more easily or is more effective than the other in reducing evil. Even if one system were dominant, that would be no reason to commit what philosophers call the naturalistic fallacy, deriving the *should* from the *is*. It is little wonder, therefore, that evil persists and that we continue to disagree concerning the best ways to prevent and combat it.

Principles may lead to rigidity and destroy spontaneity, it may be claimed, but that is a small price to pay if evil is to be prevented. They make the individual hesitate, they compel him to reflect upon the choices before him and to pass a secondary judgment. They may not suggest the immediate solution, although they indicate the alternatives. Just as the explanation of human behavior involves many interacting variables, so the application of principles to a given decision involves many *ifs* and *buts*. Then, too, the wording of principles may be learned so well that their inner meaning is forgotten, and they no longer influence behavior appreciably. Any good Christian, for example, can repeat the Lord's prayer and other principles derived from the Bible; but are these injunctions salient and compelling when he must make crucial decisions? Do they in fact tell him precisely what to do?

A most significant goal or consequence of socialization is the development of conscience.[47] To a certain extent, conscience means self-knowledge, the admission that one is not a saint and is capable of evil or evil actions. Conscience, however, can mean also the principles just mentioned: do not kill, steal, rape, lie; if you do, you will be punished, you will be committing a sin, you will suffer from guilt. An individual with a strong conscience experiences guilt or shame as he contemplates or anticipates behavior involving evildoing. He relies more on internal promptings than on the external praise and punishment administered by his family, peers, and other authorities. Without question these internal promtings can be learned, provided the society encourages rather than discourages such a process of internal rather than external social control.[48]

In addition, conscience involves or should involve a sense of responsibility. Hitler enabled many Germans to perpetrate evil deeds by proclaiming that he alone was responsible for all that went on in Nazi Germany; thus, there was no need for loyal Germans to consult their consciences. In mild laboratory situations subjects *may* be more aggressive when they are simply told that the investigator and not they are responsible for what they do.[49] To the extent that each individual actually feels responsible for his own actions and their effects upon his fellow men, he may be less likely to commit evil. But how can these pangs be ever salient when, as in a crowd situation or in government, the individual can hide behind anonymity and hence feel irresponsible?

Conscience, with or without clearly formulated principles, may induce actions that on some other standard are judged to be evil, even bestial. I am thinking of important persons, like the judges during the Spanish Inquisition, or of so-called little men in Nazi Germany who killed or arranged for killings. These individuals were obeying their consciences; they considered their deeds to be good, certainly not evil. And so while it is true that internal promptings in some persons are likely to lead to more consistent behavior (which may prevent them from committing evil deeds) than external reinforcements or sanctions, as a way of preventing evil it would appear that this pathway, though promising like all the other pathways, is no certain panacea.

Conscience implies consciousness, which in turn is affected by unconscious impulses. The Evildoer may be utterly convinced that his actions produce only good consequences and that he has only the highest motives, but unintentionally he may be performing an evil deed. There is always the possibility of a discrepancy between conscious motives and their consequences, as well as between unconscious impulses and conscious convictions.[50]

Even though it be true, as psychoanalysts and amateurs are prone to emphasize, that consciousness is a mere epiphenomenon of deeper impulses, both the prevention and combating of evil usually spring from conscious planning, for "to be aware is to know, to understand, to perceive directly," and such awareness "implies the ability to predict and control," without which decisive action is impossible.[51] Being conscious of evil is in itself not a solution, but it may be a necessary first step. A dilemma thus arises: think no evil because evil thoughts may lead to evil deeds, yet those thoughts—if they are of the proper kind—may be a stalwart inhibition against evil deeds. When the individual is conscious of his consciousness, he is likely to feel responsible for his own actions, inasmuch as "the absence of the external power expresses itself in the well-known feeling (usually considered characteristic of the consciousness of freedom) that one could also have acted otherwise."[52] In Western society the tendency to ascribe responsibility to oneself *may* increase with age and schooling;[53] and it *may* be more prevalent among those underprivileged who are proud rather than ashamed of their heritage. With a conscience and a feeling of responsibility, it may be possible to strengthen "people's capacity to tolerate irreducible uncertainty, fear, and frustration without having to take refuge in illusions that cripple their potential for realistic behavior,"[54] and thus they may be less inclined toward evildoing.

These references to socialization and conscience can be brought to an end by asserting that the promotion of the good life is more effective than principles, rules, and taboos that would prevent evil actions. It is both meaningful and meaningless, however, to advocate that every human being should have the opportunity to develop his own potentiality, for what is meant by "potentiality"? Can it be specified in detail, especially in relation to the individual's own peers (who also need their opportunities which may or may not be compatible with one another), as well as the initiative he may be expected optimally to exercise? All of us in a sense are concerned with the problem of planning institutions or with their modification. Is a caste system, for example, good or bad? No matter how defined, it limits the mobility of the individual; but is that good or bad? In many traditional societies the individual's status (including his prestige, his occupation, his choice of spouses), is determined at birth, and he is not likely to raise doubts concerning its validity or desirability. His potentiality is definitely circumscribed, but he presumably has both internal and external security. Is this good or bad?

Socialization refers to early, education to later, training; one fades into the other. The training against evildoing during the early years must continue during the later years, just as—I return compulsively to a favored illustration—the Evildoers among the Nazis may have been unwittingly conditioned during childhood, and then as adolescents and adults had their proclivities strengthened by the Nazi organization. Throughout the lifespan, therefore, the distinction between good and evil has to be learned and continually reinforced. The rationale for obeying a society's rules and hence engaging in moral rather than evil action may develop slowly and by stages. In Taiwan, Mexico, Turkey, Yucatan, and more thoroughly in the United States, it has been shown that this rationale *may* begin with conformity in order to avoid punishment and may progress as follows: conformity "to obtain rewards, have favors returned, and so on"; "to avoid disapproval, dislike by others"; "to avoid censure by legitimate authorities and resultant guilt"; "to maintain the respect of the important spectator judging in terms of community welfare"; and finally "to avoid self-condemnation."[55] Only when the last stage is reached—and it is not, of course, reached by all children or adults in the societies under investigation—can it be said that the individual is obeying his conscience, or at least this seems to be a useful, opportunistic definition of conscience.

Potentially encouraging is the fact that all of us—professionals, parents, persons with common sense—seem to agree that early education has a lasting effect upon children and adults. The basic tenets of religion are communicated, at least in Western societies, almost as soon as the child acquires language. The avoidance of evil and the adherence to good are included in the curriculum: the child is taught not to hurt others, to be obedient, to believe in some kind of theology, but not always with success or with varying degrees of success from individual to individual. At the same time, however, evil may be perpetuated in the home, the school, and the society at large. Theologians may maintain, moreover, that they seek adults who are Theologic Men and who, consequently, freely select good rather than evil and who do not automatically follow the precepts of the church without consciously making the decision. Choose the good but do so in the presence of the evil: this is a challenge that only the brave and the strong—or the dogmatic—can ever meet.

In any society the meaning of the symbols to be associated with good and evil is learned either informally or through a formal system of indoctrination. Until recently in our society and in many others, evil has been associated with darkness, which, like the night, people fear. We sleep and dream in the dark. Animals and creatures with evil reputations (owls, bats, witches, incubuses) flourish in the dark.[56] But in the United States, this association may be slowly changing since the claim that "black is beautiful" has gradually become much more than a slogan. In general terms, moreover, such associations are only a first step toward the prevention of evil; they serve to identify the phenomenon.

In later life, especially in the school, traits associated with good rather than evil can also be cultivated. But once again it is not easy to identify the traits, and new complications arise. Consider, for example, the ever-popular, highly publicized, perhaps overrated need for achievement, which its proponents believe is generally associated only with the good because they themselves happen to live in a society that places great emphasis upon achieving.[57] Even if we grant their contention concerning its relation to good rather than evil, I am baffled: that trait *may* be related to at least a dozen other traits, such as risk taking, vocational choice, self-concept, and so forth. Such findings, not convincing in themselves, suggest that this so-called need cannot be acquired or changed without repercussions not necessarily desirable from the standpoint of some other Judge.

Perhaps, therefore, in attempting to prevent evil through education, it is wise to be realistic and to agree again that there are always gradations between good and evil and that the two may intermingle in every person or situation. All of us are unlike the characters in fairy tales; we have streaks of both good and evil. The criminal gradually reforms, the solid citizen slips carelessly into crime. The sinner suddenly becomes a saint after his conversion, the lover a murderer after being rejected. An ill wind is supposed to blow some good: whatever a

Judge chooses to call good can also emerge from a disaster. In times of deep tragedy—the bombing of Britain during World War II, the arrival of the Turkish army in Cyprus in 1974—the neuropsychiatric rate may decline. Once more, we dare not be blinded by a utopian vision, however important visions are as sources of motivation.

We must not be blinded, moreover, by the Western tradition in which perforce we are embedded, for wittingly or not, we are heirs to what others before us have thought. Somewhat tangentially—but I think sufficiently relevantly—I would mention St. Augustine very briefly and most inadequately (and so let me recommend him and point out in passing that excellent studies of his theology are available, if his original words seem too numerous).[58] He attacked the doctrine of Mani for subscribing to the view that good and evil are opposites. In his opinion, since God is immutable, there can be good without evil and free will without sin. Superficially, this view seems neither striking nor provocative; yet his influence on Western thinking has been and continues to be great. Why? First, his discussion of the problem springs from the sins he himself committed in his youth so that out of his self-confessed evil deeds came his reform or conversion, as well as a philosophy of the good. He sounds human, like any reformed character, and hence from this standpoint is most appealing. Perhaps more important, although God may be immutable, persons are clearly mutable and hence they can commit evil when they oppose the limit, form, or order given by nature; they can sin when they "incline to that which justice forbids and from which we are free to abstain."[59] Each of us has a touch of that view in himself, and consequently we do not anticipate, may not even wish, perfection.

At the same time, though our reach may exceed our grasp, it is possible to imagine educational objectives that may prevent or at least diminish evil. Sensitivity to one's contemporaries for the sake of one's present or future both during or after one's own lifetime may inhibit evildoing. The individual may be thinking of his immediate family and associates or, if he occupies a powerful position, posterity in the sense of those who read history books or remember history. A small cocktail party was once given by the head of an African state for a few Americans. We had privately been judging some of his actions to be good, others evil. In the friendly atmosphere created by his truly charismatic personality, he said he had invited us because he believed his place in history would be determined not only by his own accomplishments and failures at home but also by what we outsiders wrote about him in our books and journals.

The cracking of symbols is important too. Otherwise out-groupers, for example, may be thought of as "the enemy" or as "the barbarians," without taking into account their individuality. Stereotypes concerning others may be wicked because they also ignore differences. Evildoing is more difficult when the Victim can be perceived as a human being; for this reason, the tendency to create nonpersons must be curbed. Individuals can be taught to distinguish between an individual or a nation and his or its attributes; one may dislike or disapprove of characteristics he or the group possesses but not of him or it in vague, general terms.

The kind of curriculum in the schools that might prevent evildoing is beyond the scope of the present analysis, but it is impossible not to return to one topic already mentioned in the previous chapter and closely associated with evil producing: the teaching of history. The question itself is a challenge: can history be portrayed in such a way that the students acquire knowledge of and love for their local region and indeed for their country without necessarily deprecating or indeed hating other regions and countries? Historians themselves may agree that "willy-nilly" they use "generalizations at different levels and of different kinds,"[60] that they unwittingly permit "each generation" to write "its own history of generalizations,"[61] that they may abuse their role as "guardians of mankind's collective memory,"[62] and that they suffer from a delusion if ever they think they can present, describe, or analyze all the data obtained from a given situation.[63] The fact remains, however, that by and large the books that they write and are used in schools tend to stress the manifest destiny of the countries being depicted. Anyone who is convinced that war or hostility is inevitable for historical reasons must place his faith in "really no more than [a set of] constructions in the historian's mind, to which the unfathomable and unruly past has, by arbitrary selection and purposeful interpretation, been made to conform."[64] Of course with hindsight or prejudice one can note mistakes that have been made in the past and the reasons therefor[65]; but again the notion of a mistake may mean either some objective not accomplished, while the objective itself may be considered good or evil. Simultaneously events close at hand, like atrocities, are more likely to have greater impact upon those who have experienced them directly or indirectly than they will on future generations, which may be more interested in the "ideals" of a revolution.[66] Doubtless the idea of an absolute or even a relative doctrine of history must be rejected.

Bits of wisdom in popular folklore are sometimes difficult to interpret. We are advised to prevent evil by avoiding the appearance of it. I suppose giving the appearance when one is innocent may produce an inaccurate judgment. The individual may set a poor example for others and inspire them to do evil deeds—or he may inspire himself to do so. On the other hand, his appearance may be an expression of guilt, which thus warns others that he might commit evil and hence induce them to take steps to prevent him from doing so.

If, as the same wisdom would have it, an ounce of prevention is worth a pound of cure, then the creative task would be to locate potential Evildoers before they have had an opportunity to express themselves through evildoing. When may a prisoner be paroled, when may a psychiatric patient be released from an institution, when is a street fight likely to break out between rival gangs, when are statesmen in a mood to declare war? We know these are crucial questions, but we know also that we are uncertain of the answers they can receive. We must try, however, as the police try—though not always objectively—to estimate when a given individual or group is about to let fly and then prevent the evil deeds from occurring. When is a person likely to feel so frustrated that he will vent his aggression in antisocial or aggressive action? Paper-and-pencil tests—for example, one measuring a so-called Human Happiness Quotient—seem kilometers away from locating the frustrations that can lead to evildoing.[67]

I conclude this chapter by reminding myself that evil apparently has always been ubiquitous. One would have to be an optimist to believe that eventually, however slowly, human beings everywhere can learn to improve their lot and to prevent evil or at least some evil. A psychoanalyst claims that, just as the plague was eliminated when people were taught to keep their water supply free of sewage, so they may eventually be taught to avoid war by taking adequate measures to prevent it. But no doubt because he assumes he is acquainted with man's instinctual urges, he admits that "it will take them a long time yet, and they have to suffer a great deal more in the process."[68] Perhaps, but men presumably were never motivated to continue being Victims of the plague, whereas war is not only apparently more difficult to prevent but also seems to have potential attractions or advantages never attributed to any physical disease.

NOTES

1. Reinhold Niebuhr, *The Nature and Destiny of Man* (New York: Scribner's, 1949), 1: 299-300.

2. François Petit, *The Problem of Evil* (New York: Hawthorn Books, 1959), p. 24.

3. Robert L. Heilbroner, *The Future as History* (New York: Harpers, 1959), pp. 79, 193.

4. Shalom H. Schwartz, "Moral Decision Making and Behavior," in J. Macaulay and L. Berkowitz, eds., *Altruism and Helping Behavior* (New York: Academic Press, 1970), pp. 127-41.

5. Richard Taylor, *Good and Evil* (New York: Macmillan, 1970), pp. 45-58.

6. Erich Fromm, *The Anatomy of Human Destructiveness* (New York: Holt, Rinehart and Winston, 1973), pp. 218-364.

7. B. F. Skinner, *Beyond Freedom and Dignity* (New York: Knopf, 1971), pp. 94-95.

8. Ibid., p. 208.

9. Ezra Stotland, *The Psychology of Hope* (San Francisco: Jossey-Bass, 1969), p. 32.

10. Richard Shuntich and Stuart P. Taylor, "The Effects of Alcohol on Human Physical Aggression," *Journal of Experimental Research in Personality* 6 (1972): 34-38.

11. Cf. Hannah Arendt, *Eichmann in Jerusalem* (New York: Viking, 1964), p. 24.

12. Ervin Staub, "The Learning and Unlearning of Aggression," in Jerome L. Singer, ed., *The Control of Aggression and Violence* (New York: Academic Press, 1971), pp. 93-124.

13. Justin Aronfreed, *Conduct and Conscience* (New York: Academic Press, 1968), pp. 42-162.

14. Bernard Berofsky, *Free Will and Determinism* (New York: Harper & Row, 1966), p. 2.

15. Roger N. Johnson, *Aggression in Man and Animals* (Philadelphia: Saunders, 1972), p. 166.

16. Christopher Hibbert, *The Roots of Evil* (Boston: Little, Brown, 1963), p. 55.

17. Cf. Robert N. Bellah, "Evil and the American Ethos," in Nevill Sanford et al., eds., *Sanctions for Evil* (San Francisco: Jossey-Bass, 1971), pp. 177-91.

18. Charles L. Black, Jr., *Capital Punishment* (New York: Norton, 1974).

19. Skinner, *Beyond Freedom*, p. 62.

20. Hibbert, *Roots of Evil*, p. ix.

21. G. M. Wilson, "Homicide and Suicide among the Joluo of Kenya," in Paul Bohanan, ed., *African Homicide and Suicide* (Princeton: Princeton University Press, 1960), pp. 179-213.

22. C. W. Hobley, "Eastern Uganda," *Anthropological Institute, Occasional Paper,* no. 1 (1902): 31.

23. Skinner, *Beyond Freedom*.

24. Simeon H. Ominde, *The Luo Girl* (London: Macmillan, 1952), p. 57.

25. Richard Cavendish, *The Powers of Evil* (New York: Putnam's, 1975), p. vii.

26. J. Dyer Ball, "Chinese," in James Hastings, ed., *Encyclopaedia of Religion and Ethics* (New York: Scribner's, 1922), 11: 534-35.

27. Aylward M. Blackman, "Egyptian," in Hastings, *Encyclopaedia,* 11:544-45.

28. S. G. Youngert, "Teutonic," in Hastings, *Encyclopaedia,* 11: 570-71.

29. Louis Coulange, *The Life of the Devil* (New York: Knopf, 1930), pp. 9-16.

30. L. Cristiani, *Satan in the Modern World* (London: Barrie & Rockliff, 1959), p. 157.

31. Ibid., p. 161.

32. F. X. Maquart, "Exorcism," in F. J. Sheed, ed., *Soundings in Satanism* (New York: Sheed & Ward, 1972) pp. 72-88.

33. Martin Malachi, *Hostage to the Devil* (New York: Reader's Digest Press, 1976), p. 389.

34. Maquart, "Exorcism."

35. Richard Woods, "Satanism Today," in Sheed, *Soundings,* pp. 92-104.

36. Cf. Auguste Valensis, "Satan in the Old Testament," in Sheed, *Soundings,* pp. 138-49.

37. Germain Bazin, "The Devil in Art," in Sheed, *Soundings,* pp. 150-68.

38. Robert L. Selman, "The Relation of Role Taking to the Development of Moral Judgment in Children," *Child Development* 42 (1971): 79-91.

39. Marvin H. Podd, "Ego Identity Status and Morality," *Developmental Psychology* 6 (1972): 497-507.

40. Morton Bloomberg and Sonia Soneson, "The Effects of Locus of Control and Field Independence on Moral Reasoning," *Journal of Genetic Psychology* 128 (1976): 59-66.

41. Russell Eisenman and Jerome J. Platt, "Birth Order and Sex Differences in Academic Achievement and Internal-External Control," *Journal of General Psychology* 78 (1968): 279-85.

42. Leonard W. Doob, *Pathways to People* (New Haven: Yale University Press, 1975), pp. 111-12.

43. Matt. 5:37.

44. Taylor, *Good and Evil*, p. 224.

45. Dorothy Lee, *Valuing the Self* (Englewood Cliffs: Prentice-Hall, 1976), p. 86.

46. Robert Hogan and Ellen Dickstein, "Moral Judgment and Perceptions of Injustice," *Journal of Personality and Social Psychology* 23 (1972): 409-13.

47. Eric Fromm, "Conscience," in Ruth Nanda Anshen, ed., *Moral Principles of Action* (New York: Harpers, 1952), pp. 176-98.

48. Justin Aronfreed, *Conduct and Conscience*, pp. 34-42.

49. Edward Diener et al., "Effects of Altered Responsibility, Cognitive Set, and Modeling on Physical Aggression and Deindividuation," *Journal of Personality and Social Psychology* 31 (1975): 328-37.

50. Bertrand Russell, *Religion and Science* (New York: Holt, 1935), p. 236.

51. John David Garcia, *The Moral Society* (New York: Julian Press, 1971), p. 1.

52. Irv Bialer, "Conceptualization of Success and Failure in Mentally Retarded and Normal Children," *Journal of Personality* 29 (1961): 303-20.

53. Gunars Reimanis, "School Performance, Intelligence, and Locus of Reinforcement Control Scales," *Psychology in the Schools* 10 (1973): 207-11.

54. Viola W. Bernard, Perry Ottenberg, and Fritz Redl, "Dehumanization," in Sanford et al., *Sanctions for Evil*, pp. 102-24.

55. L. Kohlberg and R. Kramer, "Continuities and Discontinuities in Childhood and Adult Moral Development," *Human Development* 12 (1969): 93-120.

56. Cavendish, *Powers of Evil*, pp. 87-107.

57. Vaugh J. Crandall, "Achievement," in Howard W. Stevenson, ed., *Child Psychology* (Chicago: National Society for the Study of Education, 1963), pp. 416-59.

58. For example, A. Anthony Moon, *The De Natura Boni of Saint Augustine* (Washington, D.C.: Catholic University of America Press, 1955).

59. Ibid., pp. 31-32.

60. Louis Gottschalk, *Generalizations in the Writing of History* (Chicago: University of Chicago Press, 1963), p. 208.

61. Alan B. Spitzer, "The Historical Problem of Generations," *American Historical Review* 78 (1973): 1353-85.

62. Pieter Geyl, *Debates with Historians* (New York: Meridan Books, 1958), p. 265.

63. Carl L. Becker in Philip L. Snyder, ed., *Detachment and the Writing of History* (Ithaca: Cornell University Press, 1958), p. 45.

64. Geyl, *Debates*, p. 268.

65. Herbert Butterfield, *Christianity and History* (New York: Scribner's, 1949), p. 99.

66. Herbert Butterfield, *The Discontinuities between the Generations in History* (Cambridge: Cambridge University Press, 1972).

67. Edgar S. Efrat, "Underdevelopment and the Pursuit of Happiness," *Plural Societies* 6 (1975): 21-25.

68. Edward Glover, *War, Sadism, and Pacifism* (London: Allen & Unwin, 1933), pp. 184-85.

9

COMBATING: EVILDOERS

The alarm sounds: evil exists, action may be called for. Who takes what kind of action? The Evildoer himself may try to combat the evil he is perpetuating. According to Confucius—a venerable if not infallible source of wisdom—he must tell the truth to himself: "The real man has to look his heart in the eye even when he is alone," since this kind of lie may have repercussions beyond the self: within the family, the neighborhood, the entire fabric of society. This means "finding the precise word for the inarticulate heart's tone" to describe one's intentions and desires, inasmuch as language is the carrier of moral principles. The self must be disciplined, and responsibility should not be displaced upon others (a form of self-deceit): "The archer, when he misses the bullseye, turns and seeks the cause of the error in himself."[1]

These are fine words, but they do not reveal the motives of the Evildoer that might induce him to seek the cause of the error within himself. Few of us acknowledge the fact that we are sinners, except perhaps perfunctorily, unless we are motivated to do so. Actually the Evildoer may find all sorts of reasons to conceal his own evildoing from himself.[2] He may define or redefine his own actions in such a way as to deny the evil consequences or his own responsibility for the consequences, or he may come to believe that his actions should be evaluated differently. The denial, however, becomes difficult when the evildoing produces adverse feelings within him. He may feel ashamed of what he has been doing or he may feel guilty. He may fear that punishment will be meted out to him now or in the hereafter unless he repents. It usually takes courage to break taboos, and returning to the fold or achieving some kind of atonement is likely to be rewarding. The witch or the person allegedly casting an evil spell is threatened and is thus driven to confess or to cease his evil ways.

Experimental research demonstrates, other things being equal—and the trite qualification is especially necessary in this instance—that the Evildoer *may* attempt to restore equity for a Victim as the magnitude of the latter's distress increases, as means to accomplish that end are readily available, and as ways to justify the evil are less convincing.[3] American subjects *may* prefer not to use self-punishment to achieve equity; rather they incline toward compensating the Victim or somehow absolving themselves of responsibility in the first place.

It is, however, society at large—which means particular persons or Judges—who respond to the alarm and seek to combat the evil or to help or to alleviate the suffering of the Victim or Victims. When do individuals respond? Evidently most persons in our society are loath to perform the role of the policeman or the reformer. We have our own lives to live and usually dislike becoming involved too intimately in the affairs of others. If the bystander is not his brother's keeper, should he be judged the Evildoer? Clearly here is an encounter with the thicket of interpersonal rights and duties of human beings. Not a single one of thirty-eight middle-class residents of Kew Gardens, New York, who heard a young woman (as she returned from work at three in the morning in 1964) cry for help for a half-hour as she was repeatedly attacked by a maniac came to her assistance nor did anyone call the police until after she was dead. They all knew her, and they themselves were safe. Later they were questioned concerning their failure to prevent the crime: "the underlying attitude or explanation seemed to be fear of involvement—any involvement."[4]

This senseless tragedy has inspired a bevy of psychologists to try to duplicate the situation under more or less innocuous conditions, some in psychological laboratories and others in actual situations. What happens when individuals are asked for money so that a person in need can make a telephone call, when they hear one person give another person incorrect information concerning how to reach his destination, when they perceive a cry of pain from someone in another room, when they observe a person steal a small sum of money, when they watch a man on crutches stumble in a subway car or in an airport, when they see a woman drop a parcel outside a supermarket, when they are told that another person is looking for his contact lens, when they are flagged by someone apparently stranded on a highway, when they are asked to telephone a garage by a motorist whose car has allegedly broken down and who allegedly has dialed the wrong number and has no more change? What has been induced from these contrived, harmless situations is that when and if Americans notice an emergency or it is called to their attention, the impulse to assist another human will not be automatic but *may* depend on a host of fairly obvious factors: their own feeling of personal or initial responsibility; the Victim's sex and ethnicity; the site of the Evil or the emergency; the nature of the request and the way in which it is made; and especially, in many instances, the presence or absence of bystanders. In addition, if the Judge himself is not an onlooker but has been affected by the situation, the reward or punishment he himself has received *may* affect his behavior. While the personality traits of the Judge *may* play a relatively minor role in affecting the decision to help or intervene, his political convictions may be quite relevant.[5] Generally a Judge *may* help a Victim in distress when the costs of helping are not too high and the costs of not helping are not too low, but in at least one situation—a real one—neither cost nor any one of the four combinations of the two costs was apparently related to the necessary action.[6] Our ignorance concerning the precise conditions determining assistance to Victims is demonstrated by the somewhat disheartening discovery that American seminarians preparing a talk on the Good Samaritan after reading about him in the Bible helped a man in apparent distress no more frequently than did some of their colleagues who were preoccupied with a nonrelevant subject; what mattered was the prosaic fact of whether they were in a hurry as they observed him while passing by.[7]

These carefully assembled findings throw relatively little light on the actions of professional evil fighters, such as reformers and missionaries. Paper-and-pencil personality characteristics, it has been said, appeared unimportant in the controlled experiments, but in a real situation those German Christians who often risked their own lives to save Jews from the Nazis during the Hitler regime, so far as could be determined, seemed to have the following characteristics: they liked adventure, they were intensely identified with "a parental model of moral conduct," and they felt themselves on the margin of society or somewhat friendless.[8] Usually in systematic investigations the Judges are made aware of the person in distress or suffering some minor inconvenience. Actually most persons, like many (or most) Germans during the Nazi era, are able to hate violently and hence to be action prone when they are at a distance from the Victims.[9] If cruelty is involved, they prefer not to perceive the ghastly details but to receive a blurred account. Paradoxically, therefore, any of us may be more likely to attack evil only when we are well acquainted with it but we also take steps to prevent ourselves from becoming too well acquainted.

It is not sufficient, nevertheless, merely to know that evil exists if action is to be taken. One cannot glance at a newspaper or television set without being bombarded with evil events calling for action. Again on a very humble level, American students were once made aware of the magnitude of shoplifting in a local store and were requested to help diminish such misdemeanors by reporting the thefts to the authorities, but they tended to do nothing to combat the practice whether the culprit (a stooge of the investigator) was a peer or a middle-aged woman.[10] The emotions of the Judge viewing the evil may run the entire gamut of human feelings ranging from sympathy or compassion at one extreme to hostility or aggression on the other. These feelings do not necessarily give rise to action, but we must assume that the closer they are to either end of the continuum, the greater the probability will be that the battle will be joined either in behalf of the Victim or against the Evildoer.

On a more theoretical level, the same conviction that justifies evil-doing in the first place often prevents intervention to combat evil: the belief that extenuating circumstances may permit departures from a well-established, even a holy, principle. "What the Chinese call a reasonable solution is one that takes into account not only the abstract principle of right (*li*) but one that gives due weight to the extenuating circumstances (*ch'ing*)."[11] The exploitation of workers may be considered necessary for the welfare of the nation as a whole. Once an exception is admitted, other extenuating circumstances seem to arise, and soon the principle itself may be jeopardized. I consider myself a case in point, I confess. I am, I believe, utterly opposed to the use of force, even when death is not a consequence. At the outset of this book I mentioned that I have been struggling with the problem of evil largely as a result of what I experienced in Cyprus in 1974 and thereafter. I ought to have a principle admitting of no exceptions—and that is often true of those condemning violence. And yet it seems to me that a people I dearly love, the South Tyroleans in northern Italy, have achieved many of their political, social, and even economic goals at least partially as a result of force directed for and sometimes by them against the Italian authorities, happily involving virtually no loss of life but the destruction of property and the expenditure of vast sums. Where, then, do I stand? If I could, would I have tried to prevent or stop the Tyroleans from using force against the Italians? And so reluctantly I am almost willing to agree with one noncosmic generalization about violence, which states that it "may be used to destroy, to control or to punish."[12] Destroy no, control or punish possibly—but surely the repercussions of using violence toward some good end may have evil consequences immediately or eventually.

The same kind of tortuous, torturing doubts arise in connection with any principle whose violation is ordinarily judged to be evil. We should always tell the truth; lying is evil. Always? Should one tell a stupid child that his IQ is low and produce an even stronger feeling of inferiority? The classic case is whether to tell a dying person that he has incurable cancer. It is so easy to find or imagine extenuating circumstances for the expression of almost any impulse leading to an evil act. Agreed, no principle is absolute. Few pacifists are so consistent that they become vegetarians; speech should not be so free—another classic—that one should be permitted to cry "fire" in a crowded theater, but this does not mean exceptions should be sanctioned willy-nilly. I recall from chapter 6 in this context the earth-shaking question of the philosopher concerning the urge to suspend an ethical principle after receiving ostensibly a divine command: "Are you really addressed by the Absolute or by one of his apes?"

The problem must persist for yet another paragraph. Violating a principle by admitting an exception must mean that the violation itself is in accord with some principle, which in turn may admit of exceptions. There must be, therefore, a third principle that can also be transgressed as a result of a fourth principle. And so on. The only way to escape the infinite regress, it has been said, is perhaps to consider all principles superfluous and to base conduct on some "ordinary feeling."[13] I consider such sophistry quite wrong. Surely it is better to adhere to a principle of nonkilling, even though there be exceptions justified on other grounds to which there also are exceptions. Why throw out a guide to behavior if it covers 95 percent and not 100 percent of the contingencies? Be grateful for the 95 percent.

What mankind seems to be doing to combat evil—and now I return to the main stream—is to keep hammering away, hoping through trials and innumerable errors to discover the most efficacious therapy. We preach to the Evildoer and ask him to mend his ways. We suggest additional punishments: the Devil is within him or causing him to act as he does, and he must fight this agent of evil by selecting a good, an approved course of action. Again skepticism must be expressed concerning the willpower of Theologic Men to make a different decision, first, because the impulses initially driving them to evil may have been overpowering and, second, because the rewards from evildoing may be even stronger. One seldom is successful in telling another person to control his emotions. "Christians regard death as the penalty of sin, the divinely appointed punishment of the crime in Eden"—but again, though everyone above the level of moron appreciates his own pending, inevitable mortality, that threat does not seem to be efficacious for many persons.[14] Members of the Holiness Church in Tennessee handle poisonous snakes, which they believe represent the Devil; hence the individual fondling one believes he becomes "a channel for God's power over the devil."[15] Here certainly is a concrete if not an effective way to combat evil.

Rather than preach to the Evildoer, it would appear more effective to attempt to evoke in him drives that will turn him away from evildoing. On the basis of paper-and-pencil research employing college students, the suggestion has been advanced that an individual is likely to follow the norms of his group only when those norms have been activated; and they *may* be activated when he has some awareness that his actions have "consequences for the welfare of others" and that he himself has "some degree of responsibility" for those actions.[16] In different words, consciousness of the ethical problems involved in evildoing must stem from a very concrete feeling regarding one's contemporaries or peers.

Without doubt most persons are susceptible to the influence of others when they are part of a unified group, even when that group is just one other person. Many, perhaps most, evil actions take place in groups or with the support of groups.[17] The remedy follows from this fact: remove the Evildoer—or the potential Evildoer if prevention is the goal—from the group that approves of the evil. One way to reduce delinquency, for example, is to change the individual's milieu in which being delinquent is the norm. On some occasions groups can be deterred from evil acts by one or more persons who have authority or who express themselves effectively; a single policeman, clergyman, or ordinary citizen may be able to restore a mob to its senses, which in less dramatic and more accurate language means combating the group's influence and restoring customary, non-evil norms. Perhaps the departed behave themselves in

Valhalla because the gods and angels in control there are the leaders and set a good example.

A danger, however, arises from this well-intentioned suggestion concerning authorities. It is true that every person, while being socialized, must learn to follow the advice of competent models. Usually but not always, for example, it is wise to obey physicians when they offer advice on medical matters within their area of competence. But there is the danger of generalization when such authorities command respect and credibility on matters "outside their narrow fields of competence."[18]

In addition, competent or incompetent authorities, such as parents, do not always function effectively as models. Whether their example is followed *may* depend upon the nature of the action they advocate, their verbal exhortation to the children, and their own behavior (whether, for example, they are self-indulgent), as well as the age and sex of those they would influence.[19] If there is a discrepancy between what they advocate and what they themselves do, their behavior *may* be more influential than their words.[20]

The timing of the communication to the Evildoer is another factor to take into account. He must be in the right mood, which in turn depends on many factors. It may be necessary to wait, for example, until some aggression has been released before the individual is willing to be attentive and hence to change.

Many of the laws in a modern society are designed both to prevent and combat evil. They concern direct and indirect attacks upon persons and their property, libel, and the issuance of false statements. Sometimes new laws are passed or old ones are reinterpreted to curb new or slightly or markedly different versions of evil. The resurgence of pornography is a clear-cut illustration. Here the assumption is that pornographic materials in some way corrupt and hence qualify as evil on both psychological and social grounds. But curbs of this sort necessarily abridge another value—freedom of expression (speech, press, the electronic media)—and therefore, according to some Judges, produce a greater if subtler evil.

Psychologically evil can be effectively combated by changing the Evildoers so that they no longer commit evil deeds. Some positive incentive for change must be offered them. They will avoid punishment by reforming, but what will be the rewards from leading the good rather than the bad life? It has often been said that the way to reform a criminal is not to rap his knuckles figuratively or administer some other form of punishment but to change his philosophy of life. It is noteworthy that major religions offer the sinner some way to repent, provided he atones for his sin and thereafter refrains from the evil action. The unlearning of stereotypes, antisocial attitudes, and evil behavior, however, is not easy. The bulk of the evidence from experience, education, and the social sciences suggests that the process in any case is likely to be slow, often painful, and probably unsuccessful.[21] We know, however, that rapid unlearning as well as learning can take place under certain conditions. In the first place, conversions occur.[22] Under this heading can be included not only those persons who see the light and find a new faith but cases like the criminal just mentioned. A violent emotional change of this sort involves the individual's basic values, and these values must somehow be evoked and placed in new perspective. The conversion may appear to be sudden, yet it must spring from tendencies that have been dormant and that at a given moment, as a result of some experience or even the word of another human being, become salient and are rearranged into a new focus. Less sweeping changes involve transformations of individual beliefs, traits, or modes of perception. The painting that seemed ugly and unintelligible looks beautiful and meaningful after a few skillful, pointed hints are given by a critic; thereafter and perhaps forever, the stimulus is viewed in new perspective. Finally, changes of a major or minor sort are facilitated when the individual is transplanted out of his normal environment, so that he is given the opportunity to be detached from normal pressures and thus to feel free to reflect and pass secondary judgments.

To realize such conditions in order to combat evil is not easy. In the area of social conflict, my colleagues and I have made efforts to intervene in two apparently intractable conflicts, one between Somalia and its two neighbors (Kenya and Ethiopia) and the other in Northern Ireland. We managed to recruit persons of goodwill (with an exception here and there) from the conflicting parties and to transplant them literally in a different environment for a period of almost two weeks. There we tried to provide the kind of instruction, largely through radical modifications of so-called sensitivity training, that might enable them to unlearn and learn habits and ways of thinking relevant to the conflict. We hoped the transformation would lead them—not us, the organizers—to think or feel differently and then either to resolve or to mitigate their conflicts and later either to communicate their proposals to policy makers or to produce associations in behalf of good rather than evil. Our successes and failures, as well as my own attempt to apply a similar procedure in Cyprus, which had to be abandoned when the Turkish Army arrived in 1974, have been reported elsewhere in some detail.[23] Here I would emphasize the supreme difficulties that arise in connection with such ventures. And I would also make one observation: the participants in the workshops we carried out or planned considered themselves, either actually or vicariously, Victims of the conflict. From our standpoint all of them were Evildoers or Victims—and the decision as to which of the two roles they were in fact enacting we left to them.

Before evil can be successfully combated, a valid diagnosis may be required. And common sense is not always sufficient. I return to the problem of violence as an illustration. Assume the following to be true:

1. Most males in a country like the United States consider violence to be evil but favor its use either as a means of social control (using the police to break up a riot) or of social change (students' demands for academic reform).

2. The advocacy of violence is modestly related to background factors such as age, race, region, and education.

3. Advocacy is more impressively related to an individual's own values (those involving retributive justice, kindness, self-defense, and humanism), as well as to the values of his reference groups, his definition of violence, and his attitudes toward various social issues.

If these assumptions are true, then it *may* follow that singling out a particular group (such as blacks or other underprivileged groups in American society) or enacting punishment through police or legal action will not be effective. Instead "good works" are needed, and they include offering meaningful proof through deeds that a group's goals can be achieved nonviolently, that justice is administered fairly, and that social change need not be long delayed.[24] Therapy of this sort is pitched broadly; for specific individuals, some of the rejected approaches may be more fruitful.

Natural situations that may be disastrous—hurricanes, typhoons, earthquakes, droughts—cannot be prevented at this stage of technological development, but their effects can be mitigated, a form of combating. The ever-improving science of meteorology is a case in point. Within a margin of error, the condition of the sea can be forecast; hence professional and amateur sailors who venture out after receiving warnings are simply not taking advantage of scientific knowledge (or at least statements of probability). If the inhabitants of a town are evacuated before the river reaches its flood peak, they have avoided evil consequences. Even with scientific knowledge, however, the unexpected may occur: the hurricane may suddenly and unexpectedly veer toward land and produce damages that might have been avoided, at least in part, if the forecast had been better. Such evils are combated, obviously, by rescuing Victims and then by assisting them—through private, community, or governmental action—to return to normal or near-normal conditions.

Social situations judged to be evil have their own perplexities making them difficult to prevent and to combat. Generally they cannot be accurately forecast for at least three good reasons: adequate data are lacking, they are complex and involve human decisions that in turn may be unpredictable, and relevant theory is inadequate. Think, for example, of the serious theoretical disagreements among professional economists concerning how to prevent or combat recessions and inflation. Again and again, therefore, modern countries endure depressions, the maldistribution of goods and services, and unemployment without finding adequate solutions. Many of the immediate conditions seem preventable or remediable in authoritarian countries—the trains run on time, as it used to be said in praising Mussolini's rule—but then the consequences of such policies may in turn be judged evil, especially by those not receiving benefits therefrom or being deprived of their own privileges. Each new regime, whether it represents a radical change from the past as in modern China or a usually inconsequential event as when one political party in America succeeds the other, tries in its way to find new solutions to benefit either the masses of its citizens or a selected elite.

NOTES

1. Ezra Pound, *Confucius* (New York: New Directions, 1969), pp. 47, 95.

2. Shalom H. Schwartz, "Moral Decision Making and Behavior," in J. Macaulay and L. Berkowitz, eds., *Altruism and Helping Behavior* (New York: Academic Press, 1970), pp. 127-41.

3. Elaine Walster, Ellen Berscheid, and G. William Walster, "The Exploited," in Macaulay and Berkowitz, *Altruism*, pp. 179-204.

4. A. M. Rosenthal cited by Viola W. Bernard, Perry Ottenberg, and Fritz Redl, "Dehumanization," in Nevill Sanford et al., *Sanctions for Evil* (San Francisco: Jossey-Bass, 1971), pp. 102-24.

5. Typical are Joel Cooper, "Personal Responsibility and Dissonance," *Journal of Personality and Social Psychology* 18 (1971): 354-63; Samuel L. Gaertner, "Helping Behavior and Racial Discrimination among Liberals and Conservatives," *Journal of Personality and Social Psychology* 25 (1973): 335-41; Bibb Latané and James M. Darley, *The Unresponsive Bystander* (New York: Appleton-Century-Crofts, 1970), pp. 121-25; and Carolyn Simmons and Melvin J. Lerner, "Altruism as a Search for Justice," *Journal of Personality and Social Psychology* 9 (1968): 216-25.

6. Lawrence M. Bloom and Russell D. Clark III, "The Cost-Reward Model of Helping Behavior," *Journal of Applied Social Psychology* 6 (1976): 76-84.

7. John M. Darley and Daniel Batson, "From Jerusalem to Jericho," *Journal of Personality and Social Psychology* 27 (1973): 100-08.

8. Perry London, "The Rescuers," in Macaulay and Berkowitz, *Altruism*, pp. 241-50.

9. Lewis A. Coser, "The Visibility of Evil," *Journal of Social Issues* 25, no. 1 (1969): 101-09.

10. Leonard Bickman, "Bystander Intervention in a Crime," *Journal of Applied Social Psychology* 5 (1975): 296-302.

11. Arthur W. Hummel, "Some Basic Moral Principles in Chinese Culture," in Ruth Nanda Anshen, ed., *Moral Principles of Action* (New York: Harpers, 1952), pp. 598-605.

12. Eugene Victor Walter, *Terror and Resistance* (New York: Oxford University Press, 1969).

13. Richard Taylor, *Good and Evil* (New York: Macmillan, 1970), p. 162.

14. Richard Cavendish, *The Powers of Evil* (New York: Putnam's, 1975), p. 55.

15. Lisa Alther, " 'They Shall Take up Serpents,' " *New York Times*, June 6, 1976, 18-20, 28, 35.

16. Shalom Schwartz, "Determinants of Congruence between Norms and Behavior," *Journal of Personality and Social Psychology* 10 (1968): 232-42.

17. Hannah Arendt, *Eichmann in Jerusalem* (New York: Viking, 1964), pp. 116-17.

18. Max Marwick, *Witchcraft and Sorcery* (Middlesex: Penguin, 1970), p. 11.

19. James H. Bryan and Nancy Hodges Walbeck, "Preaching and Practicing Generosity," *Child Development* 41 (1970): 329-53.

20. David Rosenhan, Frank Frederick, and Anne Burrowes, "Preaching and Practicing," *Child Development* 39 (1968): 291-301.

21. Leonard W. Doob, *Patterning of Time* (New Haven: Yale University Press, 1971), pp. 397-400.

22. Ibid., 400-06.

23. Leonard W. Doob, "A Cyprus Workshop," *Journal of Social Psychology* 94 (1974): 161-78.

24. Monica Blumenthal et al., *Justifying Violence* (Ann Arbor: Institute for Social Research, 1972), pp. 39, 225, 238, 254-55.

Part Four

VICTIMS

10

CAUSATION: VICTIMS

On the surface it appears as if Evildoers or evil-producing groups and situations alone account for the misery or injustice suffered by Victims. The individual is murdered by a gangster, drafted into the army by his government to fight an unjust war, or rendered homeless by a sudden flood. The evil stems from the gangster, the government, or the flood; they are the causes without doubt.

Similarly any doctrine of original sin conceives of mankind as the unwitting Victim. The sin may have been committed by one or more ancestors in some lost paradise; it may be a part of inborn nature; it may have been generated by some metaphysical event. Suffering assumes the form of acknowledging the sin and leading an existence that will bring about forgiveness, atonement, even grace. The Victim, then, is responsible not for the Evil but for overcoming it.

We are too aware, however, of the difficulty we always encounter in seeking cause-and-effect sequences among human beings. The very fact of multivariance, the many prior influences that affect a person at a given moment, should give pause before Victims are absolved of all responsibility. A challenge arises in bold form almost always when groups rather than single individuals are judged. Often careless metaphors are employed to describe such groups, as when a whole country is called "paranoid" or "guilt-ridden." But when it is asserted that a country is the Victim of a dictatorship, a real phenomenon may be the distant referent: free speech is stifled, schools are rigidly controlled, people are imprisoned without fair trials or are given no trials at all, wealth is most unequally distributed. The Victims in fact are all the citizens of the country other than the leaders and the elite in positions of power. But, the crucial question is, Could the Victims have prevented the dictator from seizing power in the first place? Why do they not now rise up and overthrow those who are inflicting evil upon them? Do not they themselves, therefore, have some responsibility for their plight?

Our stereotype tends to absolve the Victim of responsibility. We tend to assume he has been leading his own life without inflicting evil upon anyone. Slowly or suddenly something happens to him, as a result of which, most Judges agree, he becomes a Victim. Let us return to the flood and assume that the waters have descended upon his home, swept away his savings, deprived him of his field temporarily or permanently. Clearly, I say again, he did not cause the flood. But why did he originally build his house in such a precarious place? Why did he continue to live there?

Imagine four possibilities. In the first place, reasonable men did not believe the site to be precarious; records showed that the river had over-flowed its banks only once, and then in another century. No human Evildoer, therefore, was the culprit. Still today we are able to locate villains in connection with natural phenomena. Perhaps the human polluters of the planet have affected the physical environment so adversely that the rainfall pattern of the region has been altered. There would then be symbolic Evildoers since the responsibility could thus be traced, in theory at least, to unknown persons; and so again the Victim would not be held responsible. A second possibility is that the dam constructed up river collapsed and there followed a sudden outpouring of water. The dam builders who are responsible are the Evildoers. On the contrary, however, they intended the dam to prevent floods, to generate power, to provide navigation upstream, and to form a lake for recrea-tional purposes. They would not be judged Evildoers unless, being stupid and inept, they built a faulty dam or unless they fraudulently used inferior materials to increase their own profits. Would a Judge hold them responsible for their stupidity and ineptness? A third pos-sibility is that the Victim or the ancestors could have been given false information about the river when they bought the place originally. If they only had known the truth, they would not have been foolish enough to settle on land that could be occasionally flooded. Once again, there have been Evildoers. Finally, the Judge may absolve the Victim altogether when he believes that external forces have determined his plight, especially if he favors "luck, fate, or fortune" rather than "hard work, ability, and personal responsibility" as the explanation of behavior.[1] The Victim wanted to move away, the Judge may think, but an economic depression prevented him from finding employment elsewhere—and that may be perfectly true.

But the Victim himself may also be to blame for his misfortune. He may have known he was running a risk when he moved into the place; from time to time, he was told, the river overflows it banks, and therefore he was building his home and cultivating some of his fields on submarginal land. This can never happen to me, he thought; besides, he added, the land is cheap and this is all I can afford. Under these circumstances the Victim shares responsibility with external conditions. Again, however, he might be partially excused if he had been given sound advice concerning the submarginal character of the land and if his own stupidity prevented him from following the advice. Who, I must ask once more, is responsible for stupidity? The man's parents are responsible if his type of stupidity is a genetic attribute; but are they responsible for a responsibility thus assigned to them? They, too, played no role in determining their own genetic constitution. Or a socially disastrous situation can be called the ultimate causes: the Victim was raised in a poverty-stricken environment in which his schooling was inadequate.

With similar sophistry it may be possible to claim that the Victim may have played some role in his own victimization. Cruelly, the question can be asked whether the woman did not really—unconsciously—wish to be raped; otherwise she would not have opened the door. Why was the victim of a mugging in a dangerous part of town at that time of day or night? "In a sense," it has been suggested, "the victim shapes and molds the criminal" and therefore shares responsibility for the crime; he helps to make himself the Victim.[2] But not in all instances, if I may turn around and head back part way to my starting point. For many, many times it is difficult or impossible to blame the Victim. If a young child is killed by a bomb from an enemy plane, in no conceivable way can it be said that he played a role in his own death, unless one is willing to quibble and assert that he might have been in an area undamaged by the bomb had he obeyed his mother and been playing elsewhere. And also I must again ask: since the crew of the plane was not aiming to kill the child and since they were obeying orders to drop their bombs on an enemy factory, are they Evildoers? Are they responsible?

Finally, nevertheless, I would add another guess to the thesis concerning the responsibility of the Victim: every individual is a potential Victim because of himself. The beautiful woman and the handsome man evoke envy, which in turn may have harmful consequences: they are attacked, literally or figuratively, for being attractive. They are not responsible for the genetic basis of their appearance, and surely not even Satan would have them disfigure themselves to avoid tempting some Evildoer to commit rape or slander. With the best of intentions, the nation's leaders—whether democratic or authoritarian—may believe their actions are benefiting the country as a whole; yet their very benevolence may have an unintended effect upon some individual who then will try to perpetrate some evil such as an assassination or hijacking.

The reference to the individual's appearance and to his type of government raises the much more serious question of whether it is possible to isolate additional factors likely to be associated with Victim proneness. Here we move away from the problem of responsibility and approach that of causation directly. Are there conditions that prevent persons from functioning as Theologic Men in reverse so that they are not in a position to choose the course of action leading away from, rather than toward, a state of affairs in which they will be Victims?

The same attributes a Judge is likely to identify when he believes a person is not responsible for his actions are also applicable to the thesis concerning Victim proneness: age, intelligence, drugs, passion, and external pressures affect the individual's ability to prevent himself from becoming a Victim. Young children are relatively powerless and can be abused by their parents, peers, perverts, and others. An individual of low intelligence may be unable to avoid Evildoers or situations in which evil can be inflicted upon him. Whoever is under the influence of some drugs and most passions may not be in a position to resist seduction in a literal or figurative sense. External pressures compel him to submit to persons with superior power.

Other conditions likely to be associated with Victim proneness can be traced to environmental influences. The individual may be inadequately socialized—because he comes from a poverty-stricken home, because schooling facilities are very poor, because for some reason he is discriminated against—and hence he is unable to cope with evil-producing forces in his milieu. Poverty or any other circumstances that place him at the bottom of the economic, political, or social heap may make him a prey to exploitation. The common denominator here is powerlessness; the person who can be dominated by others is vulnerable. An environmental factor, now recognized as potentially crucial in the development of the individual, is birth order or a child's relation to other siblings, including the condition of being an only child. In a popular treatise by a clinical psychologist, the following statement is made, presumably concerning Americans:

> Oldest children need approval. They are susceptible to social pressure, and have a tendency to change opinions to agree with others. Confronted by authority, firstborns generally are more conforming and responsive to accepted standards than other children are. . . .
>
> Oldest children generally prefer to avoid conflict, but also regard themselves as able to change situations. However, if a situation arises which they cannot control (or believe they can't), their anxiety rises, and they seek reassurance from other people. In disaster situations firstborns tend to be more afraid than others, and seek out other people for support.[3]

If we assume benevolently that the statement is valid (though in fact the evidence is spotty and unconvincing), we can imagine that some of the traits allegedly associated with birth order may affect an individual's ability to resist victimization. If oldest children need approval, succumb to social pressure, and tend to agree with others, then maybe they can be more easily led astray by Evildoers. This *if* is sheer speculation, serving only the function of suggesting that any environmental factor, like birth order, may have implications for Victim proneness. The argument may go either way, or in neither way, but the factor itself remains potentially relevant.

Similarly, personality traits may also have relevance. Here it is not necessary to decide how and why a particular trait has developed, for the origins may be diverse and reside within a complicated combination of genetic and environmental factors. An individual with a weak ego, for example, may be unable to fend off Evildoers, or he may be willing to acquiesce since he lacks the values that could conceivably inhibit him. Another way of expressing the same tendency is to point to guillibility or suggestibility. Individuals *may* be influenced by communications coming from respected authorities, and some may be more easily persuasible than others.[4] If the authorities in question are Evildoers, then those receiving their communications will be potential converts. Again, speculation suggests, some traits may turn the individual in either direction. Rigid, dogmatic individuals, for example, *may* be less willing than more elastic or tolerant persons to accept an innovation when they live in communities not receptive to change in general, but these particular traits may play no role whatsoever when the individuals actually live in communities favorably disposed toward change;[5] and the elastic *may* be able more readily than the rigid to distinguish between the source and content of a communication in evaluating its merits.[6] Rigidity and dogmatism under certain circumstances, therefore, may render the potential Victim less susceptible to a communication when only its content is considered but more susceptible when the source is taken into account. The communication, however, may involve either good or evil, and hence this attempt to apply what we know about a particular trait leads us virtually nowhere.

Victim proneness may be correlated with certain beliefs, a prototype of which is fatalism. American secondary-school students, for example, have various attitudes toward intelligence and intelligence tests, which in fact play an important role in their careers. Those having a relatively fatalistic approach to events (as measured by a paper-and-pencil test) *may* be less interested in learning how they have fared on a particular test and may be less inclined to estimate their own intelligence as high than those having a less fatalistic attitude.[7] If an individual believes he is relatively powerless to control events and to overcome whatever it is that intelligence determines, *perhaps* he is less likely to feel capable of warding off evil.[8] I suspect that most persons in our society follow some sort of middle way, for even the most fervent believer in fatalism or free will always admits exceptions to his basic view; and the most determined determinist believes at least existentially that he makes decisions for himself. Thus one can be fatalistic regarding genetics and gravity but voluntaristic regarding personality and politics—and voluntarism may well facilitate actions against evil.

Any of the individual's own values in fact may cause him to consider himself a Victim. A member of a democratic society, for example, may feel victimized whenever he is deprived of what he considers to be freedom of choice, which may include for him the opportunity to formulate, vary, and execute plans affecting his own welfare.[9] This problem of freedom has recently been examined from the viewpoint of the Victim who believes he has freedom of choice and finds one of the alternatives blocked:

Psychological reactance is the motivational state of the person whose freedom has been assaulted. The child who does the opposite of his parents' instructions is acting out of reactance, and so is the person who comes to love Shakespeare merely because the tickets to the play are sold out. The child is reacting against attempted influence, whereas the newcomer to Shakespeare is reacting against the impossibility of gaining entrance to the play.[10]

If "reactance is set up whenever a freedom encounters interference," then the potential Victim must believe that he possesses the freedom of choice in the first place.[11] The degree to which he considers himself a Victim, therefore, *may* depend not only on that belief and its strength and importance but also on the future implications of the deprivation. Similarly it may be that nationals of one country do not judge themselves to be deprived of additional territory until some other power tells them they may not have what they had not previously sought. The desire for freedom and control of one's own destiny, however, cannot be glibly dismissed as an ethnocentric value of Western society (though it may be just that) or as an illusion invented to combat a deterministic approach to existence, for its absence not only among human beings but also among animals may create the kind of havoc or poor performance included within the psychological criterion of evil.[12]

In maintaining that sometimes the Victim is responsible for his condition and even by suggesting that some persons may be inclined toward Victim proneness, I place myself in the category of "Victim Blamer," a category that has been contemptuously attacked in a stimulating book.[13] I plead guilty, but only in part. I have said that the Victim may play a role in producing the evil from which he suffers, but I am willing to admit that the Victim who so behaves is not responsible for his role. Simultaneously let us recognize again the need within all of us to shift responsibility. One investigator has summarized his own investigations and observations:

. . . It is extremely upsetting to witness another person's suffering; however, I am much less disturbed if he deserved it—if the victim is a "bad guy" or if he did something to deserve his suffering. . . . For their own security, if for no other reason, people want to believe they live in a just world where people get what they deserve. Any evidence of undeserved suffering threatens this belief. The observer then will attempt to reestablish justice. One way of accomplishing this is by acting to compensate the victim; another is by persuading himself that the victim deserved to suffer.[14]

There is, however, a vast difference between blaming the Victim in order to retain one's fantasies or dreams and assigning him some kind of role in a long series of cause-and-effect events leading to the evil. A problem I find more fascinating than blaming the Victor Blamer is to try to discover the differences between those believing in a just world and those who do not, between the blamers and the nonblamers. Thus the former *may* be "more religious, more authoritarian, and more oriented toward the internal control of reinforcements than nonbelievers," and they may also be more likely "to admire political leaders and existing social institutions, and to have negative attitudes toward underprivileged groups"; but the believers "may no longer derogate the victim" when his suffering is "undeniably" caused by some other person.[15]

At the conclusion of this chapter I do not give the floor again to Cassandra but to Jove himself. And Jove in his wisdom, for he is king of the gods, points a javelin at me and says, in effect, Look, you have been trying to be sophisticated by turning people's beliefs upside down. You know perfectly well, he bellows without the trace of a friendly grin, that almost always in a miserable world the Victims are not to blame: they cannot avoid the hunger, the bombs, the insults, the joylessness they endure. You have been quibbling or harping on very special instances: Evildoers and evil situations are responsible for evil, not the Victims. I agree, I suppose—by and large.

NOTES

1. David W. Reid and Edward E. Ware, "Multidimensionality of Internal versus External Control," *Canadian Journal of Behavioural Science* 5 (1973): 264-71; 6 (1974): 131-42.

2. Hans Von Hentig, *The Criminal and His Victim* (New Haven: Yale University Press, 1948), p. 384.

3. Lucille K. Forer, *The Birth Order Factor* (New York: David McKay, 1976), p. 49.

4. Irving L. Janis et al., *Personality and Persuasibility* (New Haven: Yale University Press, 1959), pp. 29-101.

5. Milton Rokeach, *Beliefs, Attitudes, and Values* (San Francisco: Jossey-Bass, 1969), pp. 145-46, 153.

6. Milton Rokeach, "Long-term Value Change Initiated by Computer Feedback," *Journal of Personality and Social Psychology* 32 (1975): 467-76.

7. Orville G. Brim et al., *American Beliefs and Attitudes about Intelligence* (New York: Russell Sage Foundation, 1969), pp. 121, 162.

8. Steven M. Cahn, *Fate, Logic, and Time* (New Haven: Yale University Press, 1967), p. 9.

9. John Dewey, *Human Nature and Conduct* (New York: Modern Library, 1922), pp. 303-04.

10. Robert A. Wicklund, *Freedom and Reactance* (New York: Wiley, 1974), p. ix.

11. Ibid., p. 3.

12. Herbert M. Lefcourt, "The Function of the Illusions of Control and Freedom," *American Psychologist* 28 (1973): 417-25.

13. William Ryan, *Blaming the Victim* (New York: Pantheon, 1971).

14. Melvin J. Lerner, "The Desire for Justice and Reactions to Victims," in J. Macaulay and L. Berkowitz, eds., *Altruism and Helping Behavior* (New York: Academic Press, 1970), pp. 205-29.

15. Zick Rubin and Lelita Anne Peplau, "Who Believes in a Just World?" *Journal of Social Issues* 31, no. 3 (1975): 65-89.

11

PREVENTION: VICTIMS

Jove and common sense suggest that the best way to prevent evil is to
curb Evildoers or to try to eliminate evil-producing situations. The
action must be taken by either the Evildoer himself or someone else.
What has been said in chapters 8 and 9 concerning the prevention and
combating of evil with reference to such Evildoers and situations, consequently, is relevant here: without Evildoers or evil-producing
situations there can be no Victims. The major question that remains is
what individuals can do to prevent themselves from becoming Victims.

It is tempting to assert that potential Victims can accomplish relatively little. In myths and Holy Scriptures, evil is often overcome through
some miracle or divine intercession. We thus come face to face with the
ancient and honorable problem of determinism. Must not the crusader
against evil, whether a Judge, an Evildoer, or a potential Victim, both
deny and affirm that doctrine? Complete determinism suggests that evil
is not preventable. It is man's destiny, it is part of his *karma* or germ
plasm to engage in evil actions. Such a view means that we have no
choice, and evil will be perpetuated. On the other hand, prevention
involves action, and action means control, which is equivalent to
determining specific outcomes, at least in part. Or should not the
realistic goal be that of merely mitigating rather than preventing evil?
Lest we drown ourselves in pessimism, we might agree with a very
socially conscious novelist who has stated that "statistics don't bleed"
and hence "it is the detail which counts."[1] For this reason an effort
must be made to avoid the "dehumanization" resulting from considering Victims either en masse or as passive ciphers.

Individuals, at least in the West, have varying attitudes toward
determinism. Frequent reference has already been made to empirical

findings suggesting that emphasis may be given to one of two views concerning the locus of forces allegedly controlling behavior. One is deterministic, even fatalistic, and suggests that we are more or less at the mercy of external forces and that we do what we have to do. The other is more voluntaristic: we are masters of ourselves, and hence we and the internal forces within us largely or completely determine what happens to us. It is not surprising that in the United States, lower-class and underprivileged children *may* consider themselves more externally constrained than those from the middle class or other more privileged groups.[2] Perhaps this feeling of futility inhibits them from taking steps to ward off evil. But I admit the last clause represents a vast leap from paper-and-pencil tests and may be unfair to the underprivileged.

Attitudes toward determinism vary from resignation to a resolution to prevent or eradicate pending or present evils. Karl Marx, for example, believed that "men make their own history, but they do not make it just as they please."[3] A revolution he thought inevitable, but in 1848 he urged the toiling masses to rise because, he said with reference in effect to evil, they had nothing to lose but their chains. He thus adopted a middle position. Lenin emphasized "the voluntaristic aspect of Marxist doctrine" during the period of his revolution, for he was determined to produce change rapidly and thus establish socialism. We know that governments gather intelligence concerning the plans of other countries, and they seek to make their own plans in order to avoid being subject to attack. Then the critical decision makers, the leaders, eventually evaluate the information provided by their foreign offices and other agents. Are they fated, they wonder, to be free or independent? Philosophers forever engage in sophisticated analyses concerning the complicated issues involved in "the clash between libertarianism and determinism," as one of them has phrased it, but except in a theological sense their musings leave the problem of prevention virtually untouched.[4] It seems clear to everyone, except perhaps to many of them and to some theologians, that in a practical sense we are forever faced with options and limitations. At any rate, finite men decide to build a bridge or a cathedral to ward off natural or metaphysical evil, but they know also they have limited resources and must conform somewhat to the natural contours of the land. The issue can be pushed backward or forward, and one can ask, for example, whether the builder of the bridge or cathedral really has freedom of choice since what he eventually chooses depends upon his background over which he has never had complete control.

Does mankind wish to rid itself of evil or almost all evil? There are those who would not prevent the suffering associated with evil because, being somewhat masochistic, they do not consider suffering and being a Victim synonymous or because they emphasize the good that can emerge from misery.[5] Is such a view an expression in another form of the old saw that one should sit on a hot stove because it feels so good afterward? I do not think so. Suffering, as the Beatitudes suggest, can contribute to human happiness. To have experienced the hell of some evil action can motivate the individual to engage in good behavior and then to appreciate all the more the rewards from good rather than from evil. A story with a happy ending is a bore if all the events leading to it reveal only goodness in man or nature; it is necessary for evil to have been overcome for the ending to have meaning and to be gratifying.[6] The optimal content of fiction or drama, consequently, must be a mixture of good and evil, with good perhaps being triumphant. And what of Socrates' comment that "our greatest blessings come to us by way of madness"?[7] A mad person may share this conviction as he endures moods of depression or elation or appreciates a split within himself. Out of madness—whether the individual be mildly neurotic, violently psychotic, or "devinely" seized in Socrates' sense—may spring the best of which men are capable, their creative ideas, their poetry, their musings, and their self-realizations. The overall judgment then may be good, although the component part, the madness, seems evil when viewed in terms of the psychological criterion and out of context. But surely all great men have not had a touch of madness, however defined.

God, it may be believed, can play a role in the prevention of evil: "Lead us not into temptation and deliver us from evil." This theological plea can be made "only if there be a God, and a God in some sense outside of, superior to, and responsible for the world," and then complaints against evil can "be entertained."[8] But, a contrary view holds that after a god has created the world and mankind, he subsequently has taken no or little interest in his creation. Such a theology *may* appear in societies in which the number of sovereign groups is so small that the desire to create order out of chaos by assigning responsibility to a higher being presumably does not arise.[9]

Still on a theological plane is the pessimistic belief that existence itself is evil, and hence evil cannot be prevented by participating fully in the life of the society. According to this Buddhist view, since sorrow is inevitable, one must escape from life by retiring from the world. Nirvana is attained when all desires cease.[10]

The contrary conception may also be advocated: "Man is only truly man when he is actively exercising his own powers, only when he has some kind of control over the events that shape his life."[11] For this reason, "man must confront the underlying alienation that exists in every age, and alienation exists whenever the individual does not have a commanding view, a unitary critical perspective by which to take in hand and react to the determinants of his social existence."[12] One thus prevents evil by preventing and combating it and by believing that one can do so.

Just as the theoretically optimal way to prevent Evildoers from coming into existence is to breed persons who can withstand evil, so it can be said that the efficient way to diminish Victim proneness would be to breed persons not likely to be led astray. When we reexamine the proclivities that may be associated with such proneness, we immediately find some clues to which we may try to cling, though with no high degree of confidence or certainty. The factors grounded in heredity, such as intelligence and temperament, should not be declared completely beyond our control when and if they can be affected by environmental influences. Except in extreme cases involving bodily disabilities or defects and susceptibility to diseases, eugenics does not appear to have been or to be a popular or feasible solution to the problem of breeding out undesirable attributes. The effects of birth order and the necessary domination of children by parents, at least up to a point, cannot be controlled. Parental treatment, important in the shaping of the child, can be changed as can educational methods in general. But here we are faced with philosophical and scientific perplexities. We are acquainted with parents and teachers who are tremendously influential, but in what direction should that influence be turned and how should the goal be attained? First, we have to ask some questions: To what extent do we want children to develop traits that will make them obedient or self-reliant? Do we wish them to become easygoing and satisfied or critical and somewhat cynical? Would we eventually have them be adults who are one- or many-sided? Whatever the decision, the immature inevitably will be influenced and made more or less Victim prone.

On one objective, however, there can be almost complete clarity: powerlessness is likely to be associated with Victim proneness. We know, however, that statuses vary within every society, and hence complete equality is a senseless goal this side of fantasy or utopia. At the same time, exploitation can be prevented or at least diminished everywhere. Caste lines, no matter how much they profit those on top, usually give rise to conflict or at least envy; they can be diminished, though never easily. Individual workers in an industrial society may be at the mercy of employers, and hence they are Victims in terms of what they earn, which in turn affects the kind of life they can lead. Unionization and cooperatives, in spite of imperfections, have prevented and can prevent this type of victimization. Other socializing forces, including the mass media, can encourage the development of self-awareness and self-respect. Again preaching is not enough: individuals must be shown the way they can develop and rescue themselves.

Experience with evil is a good, if not the best, teacher, for enduring evil in the past can be helpful in the future. The Victim who has learned the reasons for his suffering will have had a valuable experience enabling him, perhaps, to find ways to avoid a repetition of the experience; he will be on his guard, since punishment can be an effective goad to improvement.[13] According to a great novelist-physician, "The greatest defeat, in anything, is to forget, and above all to forget what it is that smashed you, and to let yourself be smashed without ever realizing how thoroughly devilish man can be."[14] Victims, therefore, come to avoid certain persons or sites associated with past evils. They learn how to combat Evildoers. They lose their naïveté and appreciate the ever-present possibility of evil. Victims who believe that what has happened to them has been caused by their own skill or lack of it rather than to chance or fate *may* be more likely to utilize past experience, at least as the basis for their own expectancies.[15] But there is another pessimistic note: the knowledge of having been a victim *may* be particularly frustrating when the victim feels powerless and cannot remove the threat hanging over him.[16]

Ultimately, of course, the individual cannot prevent himself from dying, but he can follow certain procedures that are, or that his physician believes to be, helpful. He consults a medicine man or a physician when ill or regularly in order not only to alleviate or avoid pain or some disability but also to prolong his own life. He leads what he considers a healthy existence; for example, millions have stopped smoking cigarettes—but millions have not. He prays or asks the gods for a longer life or recovery from an illness, and others who wish him well may add their own voices to the plea. He prevents himself from thinking about death, directly by suppression or repression, indirectly through the use of euphemisms when reference to the topic is essential. He would transcend the inevitability of death in two ways. The memory people have of him after he dies, he hopes, will be favorable; since death itself is unavoidable, he accumulates heirs, wealth, fame, or goodwill while he is still alive.[17] Or he comes to have faith that his spirit will live eternally in some afterlife or be reincarnated in another body. Sleep, death's close neighbor, however, indicates to him every morning as he awakens that life in fact can continue in his absence; and the actual death of his relatives and friends and of other human beings constantly reminds him that he too is mortal. Somehow, however, just as many persons believe they are inviolable ("it cannot happen to me"), so he may secretly convince himself during moments of optimism that he may somehow escape the doom of mankind.[18]

A seemingly naïve way to prevent evil is for the potential Victim to threaten the potential Evildoer with retaliation. If you strike me, I shall hit back—and the strike may be the slap of a playmate or the atomic bomb of an adversary. But is the threat of retaliation effective? In our times we hear talk of negotiating with another country from a position of strength, the assumption being that the potential enemy or Evildoer will not hit us if they know we shall then hit them. But will the adversary believe that the potential Victim has the capability of striking back? The belief *may* be essential if he is to be deterred.[19] Military potential, moreover, is not easy to calculate since nations try to conceal their strength. The threat of retaliation *may* be effective only when the potential Evildoer has not been angered or frustrated by whoever makes the threat.[20]

The outcome of these devices the individual employs to prevent himself from becoming a Victim in some respect is a general philosophy, a religion, or a way of coping with existence. The consequence for him is, he hopes, a more or less satisfying way of life. He is resigned to his destiny; he prays for assistance; he superstitiously avoids certain practices or conditions; he does not walk along dark streets; he installs a burglar alarm in his shop; he takes out an insurance policy. His behavior ranges from extreme belligerency or extroversion to withdrawal or introversion. Somehow he makes a choice.

What ounce of prevention is available to the potential Victim in order to effect more than a pound of cure? One suggestion, derived from a reasonably realistic experiment, is so simple and so in accord with common sense that one is almost but not quite embarrassed to mention it. *Perhaps* one can protect oneself or one's property if one enlists the help of someone else. Ask a bystander, even a stranger, for example, to prevent a theft in one's absence. And that bystander, that ally *may* provide an effective ounce when he is not in a position to diffuse responsibility for the assistance thus requested onto another person.[21]

But the ounce by and large is more likely to be found when evil is prevented through the formal institutions of the society, provided they are on the side of the angels and not instruments of Satan. The individual accused of breaking a taboo or regulation is given a trial; whether justice is administered swiftly or slowly, fairly or not, depends on the opinion of the Judge making the evaluation. In our own culture there is a long tradition in the law that every person is entitled to a fair trial, but in practice this ideal is often not achieved. All of the reforms concerning which political leaders speak so loudly—ranging from proper medical care to some form of unemployment insurance—would prevent the kind of victimization over which most persons can exercise little if any control. Voluntary or informal organizations arise that would protect consumers from misrepresentation and fraud. Alliances among nations, such as NATO or the Eastern Bloc, seek to prevent aggression on the part of hostile neighbors. The United Nations attempts to curb the outbreak of wars through peaceful means. From their standpoint missionaries provide heathens with an opportunity to escape the evil of external damnation while also offering them tangible advantages in the areas of health and education. Again there is no panacea, merely trials and many efforts to diminish the number of Victims or the extent of their suffering.

NOTES

1. Arthur Koestler cited by Viola W. Bernard, Perry Ottenberg, and Fritz Redl, "Dehumanization," in Nevill Sanford et al., *Sanctions for Evil* (San Francisco: Jossey-Bass, 1971), pp. 102-24.

2. Esther Battle and Julian B. Rotter, "Children's Feelings and Personal Control as Related to Social Class and Ethnic Group," *Journal of Personality* 31 (1963): 482-90.

3. Cited by James Eayrs, *Fate and Will in Foreign Policy* (Toronto: Canadian Broadcasting Corporation, 1967), p. 1.

4. R. L. Franklin, *Freewill and Determinism* (New York: Humanities Press, 1968), p. 7.

5. Cf. François Petit, *The Problem of Evil* (New York: Hawthorn Books, 1959), p. 55.

6. Philip P. Hallie, *The Paradox of Cruelty* (Middletown: Wesleyan University Press, 1969), p. 63.

7. Cited by E. R. Dodds, *The Greeks and the Irrational* (Berkeley: University of California Press, 1959), p. 64.

8. W. D. Niven, "Good and Evil," in James Hastings, ed., *Encyclopaedia of Religion and Ethics* (New York: Scribner's, 1922), 6: 318-26.

9. Guy E. Swanson, *The Birth of the Gods* (Ann Arbor: University of Michigan Press, 1960), pp. 61-65.

10. Niven, "Good and Evil."

11. Ernest Becker, *The Structure of Evil* (New York: George Braziller, 1968), p. 140.

12. Ibid., p. 141 (italics omitted).

13. Petit, *Problem of Evil*, pp. 99-101.

14. Louis-Ferdinand Céline, cited by Hallie, *Paradox of Cruelty*, p. vii.

15. E. Jerry Phares, "Expectancy Changes in Skill and Chance Situations," *Journal of Abnormal and Social Psychology* 54 (1957): 339-42.

16. Hallie, *Paradox of Cruelty*, p. 119.

17. Ernest Becker, *Escape from Evil* (New York: Free Press, 1975), pp. 26-90.

18. Irving Janis, *Air War and Emotional Stress* (New York: McGraw-Hill, 1951), pp. 172-77.

19. Betsy Q. Griffin and Ronald Rogers, "Reducing Interracial Aggression," *Journal of Psychology* 95 (1977): 151-57.

20. R. A. Baron, "Threatened Retaliation for the Victim as an Inhibitor of Physical Aggression," *Journal of Research in Personality* 7 (1973): 103-15.

21. David R. Shaffer, Mary Rogel, and Clyde Hendrick, "Intervention in the Library," *Journal of Applied and Social Psychology* 5 (1975): 303-19.

12

COMBATING: VICTIMS

"What treatment, by whom, is most effective for this person with that specific problem, and under which set of circumstances?"[1] This multi-barrelled question, a variant of one that was raised in connection with communication decades ago, states the therapeutic problem for Victims in a way that clearly indicates its multivariance: no remedy is likely to be effective for all persons under all conditions. An obvious example: if the Victim dies or is hopelessly maimed as a result of the Evildoer or the situation, then combating is impossible, at least by him, if not by his peers or society at large.

When evil stems from a natural event—again the hurricane is the pro-totype—its consequences can be only mitigated. Relief is given to the Victims, literally or figuratively. Food is brought to the starving, medical supplies are dropped to the marooned. A relatively minor problem arises when those bringing assistance are torn between loyalties to various reference groups such as the family and the community. Which group should receive priority?[2]

Combating the social situations arising directly or indirectly from human ignorance, stupidity, ambition, or greed offers the same challenges and leads to the same maddening uncertainties as those discussed in connection with the prevention of evil. How do you lead a nation out of a recession? How do you improve a government that is malfunctioning? How do you get rid of tyrants? How do you stop a war? Material and scientific progress has helped somewhat to soften these evils, but millions of persons still do not have enough to eat or die pre-maturely for lack of adequate medical care. No self-appointed or peer-selected messiah, no great or petty statesman, no significant or pedantic scientist, no glorious or mediocre poet has produced for such problems the semblance of a panacea whose validity has been adequately demonstrated or even merely documented. We catch glimpses of solutions; otherwise we and leaders might be even less politically active and creative than we and they are at present. But clear-cut ways to combat the evils of most diseases have been found, and life is prolonged. The evil of overwork, if it be an evil, has been overcome in the West by machines, although they have given rise to other difficulties and have had consequences often judged to be evil.

It seems clear that a Victim is never passive, no matter what his outward appearance suggests.[3] His immediate impulse may be to relieve his suffering by striking back against the perceived Evildoer: frustration is likely to lead to counteraggression. Whether he actually carries out such an impulse depends on external conditions and the strength of his own feelings.

The ugly subject of hate among Victims thus arises. Inevitably, I think, Victims feel some hatred within themselves, particularly when they ascribe their misery to a perceived source. They hate the wind that blows down their tents and fills their eyes and mouths with sand. They hate the man who cheats them or steals their money. They hate the rival who wins their beloved. They hate themselves for not controlling some of their own impulses. Should such hatreds be included in the category of evil? The argument can go either way. On an individual level, hatred of a person may harm both the hated and the hater, and so the psychological criterion is satisfied. But from a moral or social standpoint, the hatred may be justified or sanctioned. Even then, it may be contended that, if evil is to be really combated, the hater should try to hate not the person but one or more of his qualities or attributes. Jealousy, envy, perhaps pride tumble into the same category as hatred.

Whether hatred or aggression should be expressed in one way or another or at all may be influenced by the Victim's conception of evil. "If one believes," a philosopher has suggested, "that a limited Deity is struggling under difficulties to realize ideals of worth, even weak human effort may in some measure turn the fortunes of the fight."[4] With such a view, one can help God by actively combating evil. But does the Victim in fact really submit to the wisdom of a higher power when, while giving voice to this act of faith and submission, he is really faced with misery or tragedy? Or are we dealing here only with a traditional cliché?

The Victim fights back or threatens retaliation when his frustration is strong, when the possibility of doing so exists, or when the anticipation of being punished is not great. Aggression is not expressed when one of these conditions is not fulfilled. Why, for example, did most—but not all—of the Victims of the Nazis in concentration camps or elsewhere not fight back? Certainly they were frustrated; also they were being punished. And yet they could anticipate more punishment if they rebelled; they may have lacked the means (that is, the guns or the numbers); they may have hoped that somehow they would be spared or rescued. Any prisoner under strict guard cannot rebel; he must repress or treasure inwardly his aggressive impulses.

If the Victim is aggressive because he believes he has been deprived of certain rights or property, he may battle to achieve restitution. But again the problem recurs of whether there are means available for him to do so. Are there courts in which he can try his suit? Will he be given a fair hearing? And some individuals with an antiviolence philosophy may suppress the impulse. Revenge as a way of coping with evil is frowned upon in Christian thought: evil fought with evil produces more evil. A desire to inflict pain upon an Evildoer, however, *may* not be easy to repress, although the exact quantity of pain inflicted may not be directly proportionate to the pain received.[5]

The Victim may derive some satisfaction from combating the Evildoer in fantasy. He imagines the forms his own counteraggression might take without actually engaging in action. His dreams, during the day or at night, may be filled with vengeance in undisguised or disguised form. He may come to believe in what he calls "poetic justice," presumably a state of affairs in which the Evildoer is finally punished and the Victim rewarded.[6]

Rationalization may also help the Victim feel he is combating the evil that is besetting him. Some good may come of his misery, he hopes, or at the very least his character may be strengthened. And there may be some truth in what he thus says to himself or in what others say to him. One of the best documented generalizations of social science and of mankind's experience suggests that seldom if ever do persons within a group (an association, a nation) cooperate more effectively than when they are threatened by a common enemy. Interpersonal relations within a country seem to be improved in time of war. The existence of evil on the outside stimulates those inside to perform good deeds, or at least these are the judgments they pass about the enemy and themselves.

Similarly a fine esprit de corps usually develops among persons who have experienced a common accident or disaster. It has long been said that only the real possibility of an invasion by Martians (or must one now say Venusians?) will unite the inhabitants of the earth and end wars on this planet.

Victims can hope for divine assistance to relieve their misery. Here is part, an important part, of the beliefs of those belonging to messianic cults. In the words of one theologian, "The momentary triumph of evil in history is seen as a threat to the meaningfulness of history and this threat is overcome by the hope of the coming of a Messianic king who will combine power and goodness."[7] Those who are said to be possessed by the Devil are obviously Victims requiring help. The Catholic church provides priests skilled in the art of exorcism and prescribes the ritual or therapy to be followed. Three aspects of exorcism strike me as particularly noteworthy. The possessed have a life history that includes frustration and misery, some of which seems to be expressed during the exorcism (but the supernatural odors and babbling in foreign tongues previously unknown to the Victim—*if* valid and substantiated—remain inexplicable on a naturalistic basis). The exorcist in charge, moreover, has had to undergo a period of training to acquire the necessary skill to cope with the Victim and the Devil allegedly within that Victim, and he himself suffers during and after performing the rite. It is as though it were being said, either literally or figuratively, that the crusader who would help a Victim by fighting Evil Incarnate runs very serious risks and must possess consummate courage. Third, the Victim must cooperate; during one session, for example, the priest performing the exorcism said: "Now is the time to choose. Remember! I told you. You! *You* have to choose. Of your own free will."[8] Actions such as these are to be contrasted with those of Victims who believe that what happens to them is largely unalterable because of God's will, predestination, reincarnation, or the position of the stars at one's birth.

Combating the aggressor may be dangerous not only because one may lose the battle but also because counteraggression may cause the Evildoer to inflict further evil acts. Evil may thus breed more evil. Folk wisdom in this context provides contradictory advice: fight evil, flee from evil. Again, can fleeing be accomplished? The poor and the oppressed, the men and women who are drafted to fight in modern wars, the persons who are attacked by thieves or sadists—they cannot flee.

They can perhaps find refuge in their imagination; they can repress their aggression; but imagination and repression may not be long lasting solutions. Victims may also hide their hostility to escape additional punishment and yet quietly strike back, at least in part. Persecution, for example, is said to give rise "to a peculiar technique of writing . . . in which the truth about all crucial things is presented exclusively between the lines."[9] The author thus allegedly communicates his opposition to those who might support him and who read what he writes very carefully, whereas he conceals the true meaning of his communication from his opponents who, according to this assumption, read carelessly and hence do not realize that they should punish him. Underground movements employ similarly subtle devices to escape detection and thus are able to carry on their work against those they judge to be Evildoers.

The specific kinds of action that Victims can take against Evildoers or in evil-producing situations are legion and include all manner of reforms. A useful distinction is between active and passive actions and those that are visible or invisible to the individuals or Evildoers affected.[10] If workers in a factory feel exploited and judge themselves to be Victims of their employers, they may strike (active, visible), carry out a whispering campaign against the company so that its sales fall off (active, invisible), feign illness so that they do not report for work (passive, visible), or simply work more slowly and less efficiently (passive, invisible). One person *may* inflict less punishment upon another person who has hurt him when he perceives that his revenge produces appreciable suffering.[11] A display of suffering, however, is not a certain way to reduce evildoing, for it seems reasonable to assume that an Evildoer will be moved by suffering and hence desist only when he has some degree of sympathy with the Victim, when he feels guilty for what he has been doing, when inflicting suffering is contrary to one of his own values, when the penalty for stopping is not too great, when he no longer is convinced that the suffering is a means to some end like revenge or deterrence. And we must not forget the judges and Evildoers who enjoy suffering or who substantiate their belief in "a just world" by convincing themselves and others that the suffering is deserved.

One principle is a virtual certainty: if the Victim survives and if he is unable or unwilling to express his aggression or hostility or somehow to seek restitution of whatever he has lost, then he must make some kind of adjustment to his predicament. He may turn the aggression against himself. Here we have Victim blamers who themselves are Victims. The Victim convinces himself or is convinced by someone—perhaps the Evildoer or an outside Evil Blamer—that he deserves what has happened to him. He broke a taboo or failed to make a proper sacrifice to the gods or his ancestors, and he is being punished. The consequences of his own behavior he judges to be evil, and therefore his misery now is in retribution for those deeds. He may even rejoice in his suffering because after death or in another incarnation, justice (which means nonsuffering) will be his. He may commit suicide not to escape from evil but to inflict upon himself the ultimate self-punishment.

The alternative to revenge or counter- or self-aggression is some form of self-control: "But I say unto you, That ye resist not evil: but whosoever shall smite thee on thy right cheek, turn him the other also."[12] Here the advice is not to fight evil with evil but to endure more suffering, perhaps to be masochistic, in the hope that the Evildoer, finding his Victim passive, will desist and perhaps never repeat the evil deed. Whether the Evildoer is thus affected, it may take more courage and self-control to follow the advice of Jesus ("Love thy enemies") than it does to fight back. Courage, though an admirable virtue, may not mitigate the evil and may not be effective. The Victim, nevertheless, who does not permit his aggression, however justified, to spill over into action or to become too deeply embedded within himself may feel less frustrated, and his rage may not feed upon itself. Humility may help: "Return good deeds by good deeds"[13] may be persuasive. Propitiating the gods for one's own evil deeds is another method of self-atonement.

The Victim may find psychic salvation by not considering himself, in effect, a Victim. As some psychoanalysts have maintained on the basis of their clinical (sometimes unverified) evidence, he may derive satisfaction from his misery; as a masochist he delights in torture. Or the figurative or literal slave becomes accustomed to his state; he believes he loves his master and is satisfied with his existence. An outside Judge could call him a Victim only by maintaining that, if he were not a slave, he would be leading a different existence, a happier one perhaps, or one enabling him to have a keener appreciation of his status. Some inmates of Nazi concentration camps are said to have identified themselves with the Gestapo guards so completely that they came to admire their qualities, including even their brutalities.[14] Similarly the inmates of an American penitentiary "unwittingly in-

ternalize" the codes of the institution and "identify with prison authorities (and with significant prisoners), thereby unconsciously accom-
modating to a psychic incarceration as narrow and as arid as their
physical confinement."[15]

Victims can thus become resigned to the presence or continuation
of evil. They anticipate some suffering—in themselves, in others—
inasmuch as evil is "a normal thing in the course of this early life."[16]
Evil, they whisper or shout, does not come as a surprise. It is better perhaps to admit its inevitability and to endure it patiently. Sometimes, they assert, submitting to one evil enables them to avoid an
even greater one, especially if the suffering is relatively slight. They
may believe that now or later their status will change, and the suffering
will have taught them something, will turn out to have been a good
experience. Like Job, they may "trust in the infinite wisdom of God"
and be convinced that "suffering is a trial by which God makes sure of
the loyalty of his own, as well as a spiritual training which gives the soul
maturity and strength."[17] But other evangelists advise not to fret about
evil, to fight it instead. Whether advice of this sort is a recommendation
to be masochistic or realistic depends on the amount of misery that is
involved, as well as upon the Victim's predispositions and beliefs.

Not cheek-turning but self-sacrifice may be a method Victims adopt
to be able to live in accordance with their own ideals. This is the solution of martyrs. From Nazi Germany we have the story of two men who
refused to be drafted into the SS, the branch of the hierarchy that per-
petrated many of the officially sanctioned atrocities. On the day they
were executed for their refusal, they wrote to their families: "We two
would rather die than burden our conscience with such terrible things.
We know what the SS must carry out."[18] These resisters were
acquainted with the activities of the SS, and we must assume that their
conscience, which labeled such acts as evil, must have stemmed from
some other tradition, perhaps Christianity, perhaps from their political
beliefs acquired before the Nazis came into power. Motivation of a high
sort was required. Their consciences had not gone to "sleep" merely
because Hitler kept maintaining, "I take the responsibility upon myself"
for Nazi conquests and other deeds.[19]

The Victim may also build up internal defenses in an effort to alleviate
his misery. Internally, since ultimately we are all solipsistically encased,
he may retain his ideals and self-respect even in the face of the torture

and humiliation or of a normal existence.[20] But only up to some un-
determined point, for as a consequence of too much misery or brain-
washing his resistance may crumble.

All that has been or could be said about combating evil is illustrated
tragically by the reactions of men and women confined to Nazi and
Soviet prison camps. Many of their experiences have been collated and
summarized by a nonpsychiatrist whose book provides significant insights,[21] some of which have been criticized by a brilliant psychoanalyst
who himself was a Victim in one of the Nazi camps.[22] What follows is
my own effort to summarize the material these two sources have
provided. It should be clear that many statements are contradictory for
two reasons: Victims reacted differently to the situation in the camps
perhaps as a result of their own latent predispositions, and a specific
Victim changed his reactions over a period of time.

Obviously a concentration camp frustrates its Victims in the most
basic manner. They know they are likely to perish; they are humiliated
often in every possible way; they are punished and may be assaulted
physically and sexually; they are deprived of the minimum of comforts
on even a survival level; they have very few alternatives they can pursue
and hence virtually no freedom. Under these circumstances, then, how
can they react to the frustration of their daily existence and to a
situation in which almost all hope is gone? Some of them surrender:
their will to resist is broken, they commit suicide, they break down,
they fall sick, they deliberately try to have themselves killed by the
guards, they become apathetic and permeated with despair. They
believe they can secure salvation as a result of the pain they suffer; they
think that they can be victorious through death. It matters not whether
we label these reactions masochistic; they certainly are self-destructive—
and understandable when one considers the tortures to which the Victims are subjected.

At the other extreme are reactions that must be judged aggressive, yes
aggressive against the authorities. None of the direct or indirect forms
of combat ever enabled the inmates of the Nazi camps to take command
and to break away en masse (although it has been reported that on
occasion refusals to work or cooperate occurred in the Soviet camps); it
is the aggressive motivation or effects that are noteworthy. Many Victims determined to stay alive, to survive, so that they could report their
experiences to the world later on; they would then strike back against

their frustrators, perhaps help to establish a better world. With the exception of a few who sought to curry favor, the Victims "made common cause against the S.S. most of the time." They spied on their captors, they tried to sabotage—at least on a small scale, since cruel reprisals were certain if they were discovered— the work they were compelled to carry on. There was some illegal smuggling and bartering, as well as attempts to disseminate news concerning the progress of the war.

Other means to remain alive had to be found since aggression was either too dangerous or provided an inadequate outlet. Great satisfaction might be obtained from insignificant events, such as tasting the miserable bowl of soup provided as a ration or the sheer sensation of body warmth resulting from work or exercise. Sleep provided blessed relief. One could try to adopt the role of observer, somehow thus to detach oneself from one's surroundings, in fact to try to believe that the degrading experience was not happening to oneself. Some of the Victims simply made a decision that they would continue to live at all costs, that somehow they would manage to hang on. Grasping the principle behind the evildoing or striving to keep one's inner self unchanged could be helpful. A few did try to adopt some of the personality characteristics or actions of the SS, although sometimes this was done as a form of camouflage to help other inmates. Individuals fortunate enough to have firm moral principles or convictions found it easier to exist, and they were less likely to perish. It must be realized, however, that these reactions to the frustration occurred among individuals whose general energy level was depleted; thus it is reported that the need for sexual activity virtually disappeared, and most women ceased to have their menstrual periods.

Most or all of the Victims, it is asserted, could not engage in self-pity, and "compassion was seldom possible." The essential decision that had to be made was whether to fight only for oneself (and hence to disregard the suffering of others, however guilty one might feel) or to help others. Individual differences were large. One survivor provides a gripping illustration of how some Victims found the strength to surmount the suffering of Nazi concentration camps:

The experiences of camp life show that man does have a choice of action. There were enough examples, often of a heroic nature, which proved that apathy could be overcome, irritability suppressed. Man *can* preserve a vestige of spiritual freedom, of independence of mind, even in such terrible conditions of psychic and physical stress.

We who lived in concentration camps can remember the men who walked through the huts comforting others, giving away their last piece of bread. They may have been few in number, but they offer sufficient proof that everything can be taken from a man but one thing: the last of the human freedoms—to choose one's attitude in any given set of circumstances, to choose one's way.

And there were always choices to make. Every day, every hour, offered the opportunity to make a decision, a decision which determined whether you would or would not submit to those powers which threatened to rob you of your very self, your inner freedom; which determined whether or not you would become the plaything of circumstances, renouncing freedom and dignity to become molded into the form of the typical inmate.[23]

The concern for others took many forms, however humble: meager rations were shared; seriously ill persons would be hidden or their share of the work assumed, lest they be punished or be put to death; thieves and informers among the Victims would be dealt with severely; collective action was demanded whenever feasible; even small gifts might be distributed. In fact, a humanist draws the conclusion after describing reactions in the camps that "the need *to* help is as basic as the need *for* help, a fact which points to the radically social nature of life in extremity."[24] My own feeling concerning these reactions is shared by those who have been through the experience or who have had contact with them directly or through what they have written: in the vilest of situations, many human beings can be resourceful and hence successfully combat evil.

The survivors have faced another problem. Many of them determined to speak out if they did survive, and some actually have done so. But victimization continues even when the Victims have been restored to a normal existence on the outside. First, they may experience guilt: why were they spared, while the others perished? Then the memory of their own experiences in the camps still haunts them; deeply traumatic experiences even when repressed give rise to perseverating psychic pain. They find that many who have never been Victims in their sense, though they may be fascinated by a recital of horrors, also do not wish to hear about the camps, and why should they—from their standpoint—be compelled vicariously to relive the degradation and torture? Evil in one of its too numerous forms cannot be wiped out with dispatch.

I return now to the general theme of combating evil by noting again that normally its presence is explained by the religious beliefs existing in a society. A Greek in classic times may have felt that he was born with a mixture of good and evil, which could not be altered; he might try to control his destiny, for example, by appealing to an oracle, although it could only reconcile him to "its ineluctability."[25] In the Old Testament, men were convinced that good and evil were assigned by an omnipotent, just God. Among the Tallensi of West Africa, the view prevails that before his birth, each person informs his creator what he plans to do with his life and asks for help to accomplish these objectives. When unsuccessful, he feels he is "fighting against the fate which he has determined for himself" and which ultimately is controlled by his ancestors—"submission to his ancestors is symbolic of his encapsulation in a social order which permits of no voluntary alteration of his status and social capacities." Involved in a theology is always some doctrine of destiny and determinism applicable not only to human Evildoers but also to natural disasters, disease, and—the ultimate frustration or source of anxiety—death. Just as a person can be brave and fearless in dangerous situations if he believes the hour of his death is predestined, so he can be an Evildoer or a Victim by being convinced or by convincing himself that all actions are predetermined.[26] But if he believes or knows from experience that the rewards and punishments he receives both now and ultimately depend on what he does, he is more likely to be cautious and to try at least to anticipate the consequences of his own behavior—and perhaps to be less forgiving of an Evildoer.

Perplexing questions remain. Which is better for the individual or for mankind in general: a blind acceptance of fate and hence an adjustment to the status of Victim or the voluntaristic view that we should not accommodate but combat evil with all our strength? Perhaps developing countries believing they are masters of their fate are more energetic as they rapidly enter the modern world, with its machinery, gadgets, and scientific knowledge. But, except for the prolongation of life, is rapid entry really an advantage and, if so, on the basis of which criteria?

Is it better to have a formal creed, which one is taught and which one accepts, than to be able to make one's own interpretation of evil? One has the impression that among traditional peoples there is room for little doubt. As an extremely astute anthropologist once remarked, in the society she studied in its more or less original state no one ever asked a question to which a stereotyped answer was not at hand.[27] There, for better or worse, one accepted one's destiny. In contrast there is no universal schema prevailing among Western peoples. Although each religion provides its own set of answers, only the most devout among us can fail to recognize the existence of competing creeds or viewpoints. The very presence of a formal discipline, philosophy, dedicated to questioning the basic assumptions of our existence must give rise to doubts among all who are affected by philosophical thinking. Daily instruction in the tenets of religion and Sunday sermons indicate the need that is felt to reinforce one particular version of fate and evil rather than another. Under these circumstances there is stimulating confusion, and men must choose. Are they any happier or more satisfied when the choice, the final choice, is at least partially theirs? Is it better to believe that the outbreak of a war is God's will or the result of the machinations of evil men?

Is the official version of fate and of evil actually accepted in full faith and belief by the disciples? When a beloved dies, must there not be moments of doubt, even among the devout concerning the wisdom of whether God's will is thus being done? When storms are attributed to evil spirits, does not the sailor try to reach land as quickly as possible or the cultivator seek to shield his crops from its most damaging effects? Eventually the faithful may return to the fold and thus survive the agony of doubt and skepticism. The doubt and the skepticism arise, I suppose, as a result of external events and of changes within us. They are stimulated by advancing age when we come ever more to weigh our accomplishments and our shortcomings and to appreciate more deeply our own approaching death. Finally, every thinking person must somehow become reconciled to the presence of evil. No explanation is completely satisfactory, none is completely unsatisfactory. We live within ourselves; we hope.

NOTES

1. Gordon L. Paul, "Strategy of Outcome Research in Psychotherapy," *Journal of Consulting Psychology* 31 (1967): 109-19.

2. Lewis M. Killian, "The Significance of Multiple-Group Membership in Disaster," *American Journal of Sociology* 57 (1952): 309-17.

3. Philip P. Hallie, *The Paradox of Cruelty* (Middletown: Wesleyan University Press, 1969), p. 136.

4. Walter Goodnow Everett, *Moral Values* (New York: Holt, 1918), p. 409.

5. Bob Helm, Thomas V. Bonoma, and James T. Tedeschi, "Reciprocity for Harm Done," *Journal of Social Psychology* 87 (1972): 89-98.

6. William Chase Greene, *Moira* (Cambridge: Harvard University Press, 1944), pp. 7-8.

7. Reinhold Niebuhr, *The Nature and Destiny of Man* (New York: Scribner's, 1949), 2: 19.

8. Malachi Martin, *Hostage to the Devil* (New York: Reader's Digest Press, 1976), p. 318.

9. Leo Strauss, *Persecution and the Art of Writing* (Glencoe: Free Press, 1952), p. 25.

10. Jan M. Howard, and Robert H. Somers "Resisting Institutional Evil from Within," in Nevill Sanford et al., eds., *Sanctions for Evil* (San Francisco: Jossey-Bass, 1971), pp. 264-89.

11. Russell G. Green, "Perceived Suffering of the Victim as an Inhibitor of Attack-Induced Aggression," *Journal of Social Psychology* 81 (1970): 209-15.

12. Matt. 5:39.

13. Ezra Pound, *Confucius* (New York: New Directions, 1969), p. 260.

14. Bruno Bettelheim, "Individual and Mass Behavior in Extreme Situations," *Journal of Abnormal and Social Psychology* 38 (1943): 417-52.

15. Lewis Merkin, Jr., *They Chose Honor* (New York: Harper & Row, 1974), p. xxiii.

16. François Petit, *The Problem of Evil* (New York: Hawthorn Books, 1959), p. 132.

17. Ibid., p. 43.

18. Hannah Arendt, *Eichmann in Jerusalem* (New York: Viking, 1964), p. 104.

19. Fritz Redl, "The Superego in Uniform," in Sanford et al., *Sanctions for Evil*, pp. 93-101.

20. Hallie, *Paradox of Cruelty*, p. 92.

21. Terrence Des Pres, *The Survivor* (New York: Oxford University Press, 1976).

22. Bruno Bettelheim, "Reflection: Surviving," *New Yorker*, August 2, 1976, 31-36, 38-39, 42-52.

23. Viktor E. Frankl, *From Death-Camp to Existentialism* (Boston: Beacon Press, 1959), pp. 65-66.

24. Des Pres, *The Survivor*, p. 136.

25. Meyer Fortes, *Oedipus and Job in West African Religion* (Cambridge: Cambridge University Press, 1959), pp. 11-15.

26. Jean Guitton, *Histoire et destinée* (Paris: Desclee de Brouwer, 1970), p. 137.

27. Margaret Mead, *New Lives for Old* (New York: Morrow, 1956), p. 85.

INDEX

Entries after authors' names refer both to the Notes where they are listed and to the pages in the text where they are cited or quoted.

About the Author

Leonard W. Doob, Senior Research Scientist and Sterling Professor of Psychology, emeritus, at Yale University, specializes in social psychology. He has published extensively in journals, and his previous books include *Pathways to People, Patterning of Time, Patriotism & Nationalism, Communication in Africa, Becoming More Civilized, The Plan of Men, Frustration and Aggression, Social Psychology, Public Opinion and Research.* He is currently writing a book on peace research.